T0206664

# ONE
## *mindful*
# DAY
## *at a* TIME

## Companion
**PRESS**

*Companion Press is dedicated to the education and support of both the bereaved and bereavement caregivers. We believe that those who companion the bereaved by walking with them as they journey in grief have a wondrous opportunity: to help others embrace and grow through grief—and to lead fuller, more deeply-lived lives themselves because of this important ministry.*

For a complete catalog and ordering information, write, call, or visit:

Companion Press | The Center for Loss and Life Transition
3735 Broken Bow Road | Fort Collins, CO 80526
(970) 226-6050 | www.centerforloss.com

# ONE
*mindful*
# DAY
*at a* TIME

*365 meditations for living in the now*

ALAN D. WOLFELT, PH.D.

Companion Press is an imprint of the Center for Loss and Life Transition,
3735 Broken Bow Road, Fort Collins, Colorado 80526.

24   23   22                                    5   4   3   2

ISBN:  978-1-61722-263-4

*In memory of the existential psychologist Rollo May,
who inspired me with his words, "The confronting of death
gives the most positive reality to life itself. It makes the
individual existence real, absolute, and concrete.
My awareness of this gives my existence and what
I do each hour an absolute quality."*

*Reflecting on these powerful words has helped
me understand the critical importance of
living in the now. I hope I have modeled this
profound truth for my family and those I mentor
through my writings and teachings.*

# WELCOME

Thank you for picking up this book. I wrote it to both invite and inspire you to live and love fully, one precious day at a time.

As I imagine you are aware, there is a significant difference between existing and living. Too many people sleepwalk through life—some even being among what I call "the living dead." Weeks pass, months pass, years pass, and still they've done little to investigate and feed the flame inside them—a flame lit by the sparks of passion and purpose we're all born with.

To me, living mindfully is about training our awareness to give attention to our divine sparks—"that which gives life meaning and purpose." Our awareness then becomes a tool for interacting with the world in ways that feed our souls. If we live intentionally each day, we create a rich life of purpose.

Mindfulness is about enjoying life and making the most of it. It's about relishing our precious time on earth. But it's also about using our discerning awareness each day to make constructive choices.

Some mindfulness gurus believe that living in the now is only about this moment. They advocate unattachment, which is a Buddhist concept of letting go of all feelings of desire and disappointment. In this practice, you work to live moment-to-moment, and you experience life, whatever happens, with no feelings of attachment to any of it. Nor do you dream up and pursue big goals, for those are considered deceptions of the ego.

You will discover a different brand of mindfulness in this book. The short version of my life story will help you understand why.

When I was in my early teens, I experienced a series of losses that had a tremendous impact on my life. Among those losses were the deaths of a good friend and my two grandmothers. Somewhere in my being I knew I needed to actively mourn those deaths, yet nobody wanted to talk to me about them. In other words, I was a "forgotten mourner."

I felt sad, mad, confused and alone. I wrote a mission statement at age sixteen expressing my desire to create a Center for Loss to help grieving children, teens, adults, and families. I'd discovered my passion and a deep, abiding sense of purpose.

I attempted to learn about grief from the ground up. I worked in a cemetery, then a funeral home, then pursued thirteen years of higher education that focused on life transitions, grief, and the need to authentically mourn. Then, thirty-two years ago, I founded the Center for Loss and Life Transition.

Since that time, I have worked with and learned from thousands of families impacted by life losses. I have had the opportunity to write a number of books on grief. I'm humbled by the many invitations I get to travel the world each year speaking about the natural and necessary need to mourn in ways that foster hope and healing. I can't imagine a more fulfilling career.

As you can see, I've been around death, grief, and loss since my early teens. I turn sixty-three years of age the very week I'm writing these words. And so—it is from this unique vantage point that I'm writing to you today.

My caregiving life, surrounded as it is by death, has made me hyperaware of my own mortality. That's a good thing, because it turns out that befriending death can help all of us get the most out of life. The more we keep one eye on death, the more authentic and meaningful our life and living can be.

Over and over again, death has taught me that life is a fantastic opportunity. It's a smorgasbord of delights, and it presents all of us with possibilities to build loving relationships and meaningful accomplishments. It's replete with joy and yes, heartbreak. Yet, whether we truly experience all of that—the delights, the relationships, the accomplishments, the joy, the heartbreak—depends on our willingness and dedication to intentional, mindful living, one day at a time. We've got to *carpe* the heck out of every *diem*.

To that end, I encourage you to read each day's entry when you awaken each morning. Doing so will help you focus on your mindfulness skills and practice them each and every day.

In the now,

Alan D. Wolfelt

# JANUARY 1

*"Now is the future you promised yourself last year, last month, last week. Now is the only moment you'll ever really have. Mindfulness is about waking up to this."*

— Mark Williams

Traditionally, New Year's Day is a day of reckoning. It's the one day each year that's culturally set aside for considering the year before and envisioning the year ahead. Well, that and watching football… In other words, today is supposed to be a planning day.

But what Mark Williams is saying in the quote above is that projecting the future and living mindfully today can be at odds with one another. If we spend too much time and energy making promises to ourselves about next week, next month, and next year, we're not fully living *this* moment.

So today, let's resolve to wake up to what's right in front of us. Let's savor each moment of football, family time, feasting, relaxation—or whatever the day brings. At least for today, let's worry about tomorrow, tomorrow.

*Now is the only moment I'll ever really have.*
*I am mindful of this.*

# JANUARY 2

*"Awareness is the greatest agent for change."*
— Eckhart Tolle

When we are aware, we are paying attention to whatever we are thinking, feeling, or doing. We may also be really and truly focusing on what our five senses are bringing in. We are not just hearing, but listening. We are not just seeing, but looking.

Imagine awareness as a flashlight. In any moment, we can choose to shine the flashlight wherever we want. If we want to bring awareness to an emotion we may be having, we turn our attention to it, fully experience it, and, importantly, ask ourselves why we are feeling it.

If there is something we want to change in our lives, our flashlight of awareness is a powerful tool. By shining the flashlight on it so we can acknowledge and examine it, we are opening the door to heightened understanding and more effective ways of being.

*My awareness is a powerful tool.*
*Its light can reveal my life to me.*

# JANUARY 3

*"You should sit in meditation for twenty minutes every day—
unless you're too busy. Then you should sit for an hour."*

— Old Zen adage

On the path to mindfulness, meditation is a powerful tool. It
teaches you to empty your mind of its incessant thoughts and
worries and instead simply exist and breathe.

If you're a beginner, just sit in a comfortable chair, close your
eyes, and focus on your breath. Counting sometimes helps.
Count one, two, three, etc. on your in-breath, until you're
naturally "full" of air, hold for a count of one, then count your
out-breath one, two, three, etc. until you're naturally depleted of
air. Or you can breathe in to a short, silent phrase, such as
"All is well," and breathe out to a different short phrase,
such as "Everything belongs."

I'll admit: I myself am guilty of thinking I'm too busy to
meditate, which probably means I really need to meditate.
I'll commit to five minutes a day if you will.
Maybe we can work our way up to twenty.

*A few minutes of meditation each day enhances all the hours.*

# JANUARY 4

*"I got the blues thinking of the future, so I left off and made some marmalade. It's amazing how it cheers one up to shred oranges and scrub the floor."*

— D.H. Lawrence

It's natural to worry, but many of us worry too much. We spend hours each day mired in our "what if?" thinking. What if this happens? What if that happens? What if both things happen and then this third thing happens? Oy.

Worry is the opposite of mindfulness.
If you are mindful, you are here, now. If you are worrying, you are living in a predicted, theoretical future.

One surefire antidote to worry about the future is hands-on activity today. When you feel yourself slipping into worry, engage your body. Go for a walk and place your awareness on the sights and sounds. Grab a broom and sweep. Putter in the garden. Cook. Knit. Fish. Play solitaire—with real cards!

*When I feel myself slipping into worry,*
*I will shift with purpose to a hands-on activity.*

# JANUARY 5

*"Some moments are for Instagram, some are just for the moment itself. I've learned to really live my life and not worry so much about documenting every split second of it. The most magical, exquisite, spontaneous things happen when there is no time to grab your phone. I wish you a lifetime of moments too beautiful to capture on film."*

— Taylor Swift

Social media is all about connecting and sharing…with people who are not here. Yes, I agree it's important to keep in touch with those we love but may not have the opportunity to see often, but do we really need to share photos and random thoughts with them multiple times a day?

Our lives happen in the now, but when we constantly try to document the now, we cut our nows short. If we immerse ourselves in an experience for five seconds then spend ten seconds getting a good pic of it then another 15 seconds commenting and uploading…we've just spent five seconds in the now and 25 seconds on documentation and sharing. Not a great ratio.

The next time you feel the urge to whip out your phone and document something, resist it. Instead, focus your awareness even more intensely on the experience itself. Notice how you feel.

---

*Experiencing the now of my life is much more essential than documenting the now of my life. I can't do both.*

# JANUARY 6

*"People living deeply have no fear of death."*

— Anaïs Nin

What does it mean to live deeply? To me it means to authentically experience each moment as it unfolds, to reach out to others to strengthen connections, and to pursue our passions with gusto and persistence. If we are doing these three things, is it true, as author Anaïs Nin said, that we will no longer fear death?

First, living deeply allows less time for worry. We're simply too busy participating in this world to be overly concerned about what comes next. And second, fear of death often goes hand-in-hand with regret. When we regret things we've done, we sometimes fear going to our graves without having made things right. And when we regret things we *haven't* done but yearn to, we sometimes fear death will take us before we've had the chance. In both of these cases, living deeply as defined above largely eliminates regret.

So yes, I agree that living deeply helps tame our fear of death. If we make our lives epic and joyful adventures, we're putting death where it belongs for now—not in the trunk but in the backseat. We're not pretending it's not there; we're just not putting it behind the wheel yet.

*Living deeply helps me befriend death.*

# JANUARY 7

*"Your breathing. The beating of your heart.*
*The expansion of your lungs. Your mere presence is*
*all that is needed to establish your worth."*

— Iyanla Vanzant

Low self-esteem can hamper mindful living. That's because deep down, some people don't feel worthy of the beauty, joy, and grace life lays at their feet every day.

Have you ever walked by a shop or restaurant and thought, "That's lovely, but it's too nice for me"? Have you ever yearned to try something then thought, "But I'm not smart/coordinated/handsome/good enough"?

I'm here to tell you that just by being born into this fantastic world, you *are* good enough. You *do* deserve whatever you are drawn to. Each day, choose to follow your desires. Be vulnerable. Take chances. You are as rightful a recipient of the fruits of life and love as anyone who has ever walked the planet.

*I am deserving of everything I desire.*

# JANUARY 8

*"Practicing mindfulness involves a willingness to be touched by life, and that requires courage. We so want to control our experience so that it's pleasant. That's habit mind. Some of us enlist mindfulness to that end. If only we can be mindful enough, difficulties won't arise. You need the courage to ride the elephant."*

— Ed Halliwell

Oh boy is *this* an essential point! Mindfulness is not the same thing as control. It's easy to get lured into thinking that if we are mindful, we can stay on an even keel. We might believe that when bad things happen—and they will—we can simply train ourselves to focus on the miracle of the flowers in our garden or immerse ourselves in meditation and everything will be just fine.

On the contrary, I agree with Ed Halliwell that true mindfulness means having the courage to be touched by life. When someone we love dies, for example, we live in the now of our grief. We hurt, and we embrace the hurt. When a loved one has a health scare, we honor our fearful thoughts and feelings.

Being mindful means that no matter what this day brings, we will encounter it authentically and fully. We will have the courage to ride the elephant.

*I have the courage to be touched by life.*
*I want to ride the elephant.*

# JANUARY 9

*"In a true you-and-I relationship, we are present mindfully, non-intrusively, the way we are present with things in nature. We do not tell a birch tree that it should be more like an elm. We face it with no agenda, only an appreciation that becomes participation."*

— David Richo

Mindfulness in our relationships with others can be even more challenging than solo mindfulness. And yet, perhaps you agree with me that love and connection give our lives the most meaning. This means, of course, that learning to live in the now *with others* may be the pinnacle of our practice.

To be present mindfully to others requires both attention and non-judgment. We set aside our electronics and distractions, we look the other person in the eye, we lean in, and we actively listen. We appreciate the person's uniqueness, and we express empathy for what she is saying and feeling. We also refrain from any critical evaluations, expressed or unexpressed, of her appearance, ideas, behaviors, etc.

David Richo's suggestion that we work on being present to people as we are to trees is a good one. Whenever we are with loved ones, let's try to remember this.

*I am mindfully attentive to others. I spend time in the now with them without judgment or expectation.*

# JANUARY 10

*"There's only one reason why you're not experiencing bliss
at this present moment, and it's because you're thinking or
focusing on what you don't have… But right now you have
everything you need to be in bliss."*

— Anthony de Mello

What might prevent you from living mindfully today? For many
of us, it comes down to the concept of *lack*. We're thinking
about something we don't have (or don't have enough of). We're
obsessing about something we want. We're worried we're missing
out on essential news, gossip, trends, social happenings, etc.

We don't like this feeling of lack, so we spend lots of time,
energy, and money scheming and strategizing to minimize it.
We buy stuff. We buy more stuff. We spend hours
every day consuming media.

But are we any happier because of this mindless pursuit
of abundance? What if today we focus on enjoying the
bounty we *do* have instead?

*Right now I have everything I need to be in bliss.
I lack nothing essential.*

# JANUARY 11

*"Life is movement. The more life there is, the more flexibility there is. The more fluid you are, the more you are alive."*

— Arnaud Desjardins

Sometimes we confuse mindfulness with stasis. We picture the ancient guru perched in the lotus position on a mountain ledge, unmoving and meditating for years on end. But while meditation and calm awareness are one face of mindfulness, another is full-tilt engagement with life.

If you're fully absorbed in a game of tag with your kids, you're living mindfully. If you're changing jobs or relocating because that's where your heart is leading you, you're living mindfully. If you're immersing yourself in foreign places or new experiences of any kind, you're living mindfully.

I agree: Life is movement. Change, though it can be challenging, is life's default setting. Learning to stay fluid and roll with the punches is mindfulness in action.

*The more fluid I am, the more alive I am.*

# JANUARY 12

*"Be kind whenever possible. It is always possible."*
— Dalai Lama

Mindfulness and kindness go together like soil and seed.

If we are fully present, living in this moment and this moment only, we are less likely to be summoning old hurts and grievances. In other words, we've left our old baggage behind us, and we're approaching each new situation with openness and equanimity. We're also working on being egoless. We have no expectations or me-me-me demands.

It is in this fertile soil that kindness blooms.
We can respond with empathy, appreciation, and good humor almost no matter what happens. Those around us are bolstered by our kindness, and they are more likely to pay it forward to people in their sphere of influence.

And just like that, we've helped make the world a better place.

*Mindfulness makes me kinder.*

# JANUARY 13

*"When we perform an act mindfully—be it meditating, vacuuming, or playing Scrabble with a child—we nourish ourselves as well. Rather than scattering our concentration on a dozen things at once, we focus. We slow down. We may not get as much done by day's end, but we can feel more peaceful and satisfied with the work itself. That's a good way to think of it: Mindfulness is quality time for the soul."*

— Shana Aborn

It doesn't matter what we are doing. If we are doing it mindfully, we are living in the now and we are experiencing quality time.

You've probably noticed by now that human existence is not joy after joy after joy after joy. If we gathered up all the most deliriously joyful moments of our lives—special family times, memorable days with our significant others, the births of our children—and cut out the rest, how many days would we be holding? Not that many.

Mindfulness makes all the day-to-day stuff more special. It elevates the ordinary to the extraordinary. It awakens us to the millions of miracles hiding in plain sight.

*Whatever I am doing, I will do it mindfully.
Mindfulness is quality time for my soul.*

# JANUARY 14

*"When someone is going through a storm, your silent presence is more powerful than a million empty words."*

— Thema Davis

Presence is rare and powerful, all right. Actually, it's a synonym for living mindfully, so this entire book is about presence and all the ways that practicing it can make life richer for you and everyone around you.

When someone you care about has experienced a significant loss or is going through a rough patch, the very best way you can help them is by simply being there. You don't have to say the right thing or even anything at all. You don't have to do anything in particular. You just have to show up, stick around, and be willing to pay attention to them and actively listen if they want to talk.

You see, we need each other, especially when we're suffering. We need love and compassion. We need the presence of those who care about us. You can be that presence for someone and in doing so, transform hurt into healing.

*How can I help my friends and family? By being present to them.*

# JANUARY 15

*"How we spend our days is, of course, how we spend our lives."*
— Annie Dillard

This admonition reminds us that each day is important. After all, how we choose to spend today and tomorrow and the day after that will determine how we spend our lives.

What matters most to you? Make a list with three columns: Lifelong, Ten Years, This Year. In each column, write down what really and truly matters to you—things you would really regret not having done in each timeframe.

Now pick two or three items in your "This Year" list and take a baby step toward each of them today.

*How I spend my days is how I spend my life.*

# JANUARY 16

*"When in doubt, make a fool of yourself. There is a microscopically thin line between being brilliantly creative and acting like the most gigantic idiot on earth. So what the hell, leap."*

— Cynthia Heimel

Why don't we try new things? Why don't we reveal what's in our heart of hearts? Why don't we pursue our dreams? Because we're afraid. We're afraid to fail. After all, what if we're bad at whatever it is? What if people make fun of or reject us? We don't like the feeling of uncertainty. It's safer not to take the risk.

Yet our daily commitment to mindfulness requires honesty. If we're consulting and staying aware of our inner voice, we know what we want. We know what feels right. Ignoring or overriding this voice, then, is a betrayal. When we betray ourselves, we are not being mindful. We are not living in the now. Instead, we're discarding the fruits of our awareness and withholding our true selves from the now.

So let's muster the courage to be true to ourselves. Let's make the leap.

*I have the courage to be true to myself. I will leap.*

# JANUARY 17

*"People attain worth and dignity by the multitude
of decisions they make from day to day."*
— Rollo May

How many decisions have you made already today? More than
you assume you have, I'll wager. You decided to open your
eyes. You decided to get out of bed. You stretched, perhaps.
You opted to make your bed—or not. Maybe you petted your
companion animal. You picked up your phone, tablet, or
computer and handled dozens more quick decisions. All this
before even leaving your bedroom.

Mindful living involves cultivating our awareness that each of
these activities is in fact a choice. Pretty much everything we do
throughout the day is a decision we can make more thoughtfully.

Too often we get lulled into mistaking routine for necessity.
For example: "But I *have* to go to work this morning…" That
may be true, but do you have to go to *that particular* job? Not
if you don't like it. And do you really have to drive there?
Could you bike instead? And if you do have to drive, could
you use your car time in a more peaceful or purposeful way,
such as listening to music that inspires you or learning a foreign
language? The more intentional we are about every choice we
make, the more mindful our days—and our lives.

*I will be more intentional about all the little
decisions that make up my day.*

# JANUARY 18

*"Restore your attention or bring it to a new level by dramatically slowing down whatever you're doing."*
— Sharon Salzberg

The older I get, the more impressed I become by slowness. And it's not just because I'm getting slow myself!

Often, slower is just plain better. A meal prepared and eaten slowly is a sensual feast. A personalized funeral planned with care and carried out over several days is more effective at helping people mourn and heal.
A book read aloud is a memorable experience.

When you intentionally slow something down, you short-circuit the automaticity and mindlessness of your usually speedy way of doing it. You force your brain and your body to consider each part anew and really experience it. Today, purposefully slow-mo something you usually do quickly and notice what happens.

*Often, slower is better.*
*To make a task mindful, I will slow it down.*

# JANUARY 19

*"Each one of us, I believe, is a gift the earth is giving to itself now, a unique gift. You don't need to be extraordinary. If the world is to be healed through human effort, I am convinced it will be by ordinary people, people whose love for this life is even greater than their fear."*

— Joanna Macy

Do you ever despair at terrible things happening out there in the world? Do you want to participate in making the world a better place? Mindfulness is the answer. If everyone learned to escape the prison of ego and live in full awareness, war would end. Climate change would be reversed. Hunger and disease would be eradicated. Innovation would flourish.

Start with yourself. Live in the now today. Live in the now tomorrow. Model heightened consciousness for your family and others. They will be drawn to your way of being, and they, too, will begin to live more mindfully. Act with awareness and intention when you reach out to support your community.

You don't need to be extraordinary.
You just need to be mindfully you.

*I don't need to be extraordinary.*
*Ordinary, mindful me is a gift to the world.*

# JANUARY 20

*"Don't seek, don't search, don't ask, don't knock, don't demand—*
*relax. If you relax, it comes. If you relax, it is there.*
*If you relax, you start vibrating with it."*

— Osho

As you make your way through this book, you will find
that I generally support an active approach to living in the now.
Go out and seize the day instead of sitting still and assuming
the day will come to you. Here spiritual guru Osho is
challenging my way of thinking, however. He tells us to
relax and open ourselves to the path of least resistance
and effortless synchronicities.

Osho isn't the only one. Many spiritual leaders believe that effort
is wasted energy. Instead, they say, you should simply imagine
and ask for what you want, and the universe will conspire to
bring it to you. Who wouldn't want that?
The "law of attraction," as it is often called, is seductive,
and I don't doubt it can be an ally.

How about this: Give both the active and the passive
methods of pursuing your goals a try.
See what combination works best for you.

---

*Sometimes things come easier to me when I relax.*

# JANUARY 21

*"If you concentrate on finding whatever is good in every situation, you will discover that your life will suddenly be filled with gratitude, a feeling that nurtures the soul."*

— Rabbi Harold Kushner

While living in the now means acknowledging and embracing whatever we're experiencing—"good" or "bad"—a lot of the time the quest for mindfulness challenges us to appreciate the ordinary. Trouble is, our minds get bored with ordinary. We don't even really notice the things, people, and activities that populate our daily lives. But what if we train ourselves to look constantly for the good or miraculous?

Let's say we're in line at the grocery store. We're not thrilled to be there in the first place. We might be even more annoyed if it's taking too long. What are we doing? We're likely chomping at the bit or playing with our phones.

But then we remind ourselves to notice the good. We look around to see if we know anyone nearby. We smile at the baby across the aisle. We help the elderly man behind us who's struggling to position his cart. We marvel at the variety of candy bars and new gum we haven't tried. We greet the checker and strike up a conversation. We celebrate the fact that grocery stores exist. We are filled with gratitude, and this feeling nurtures our soul.

*I will look for the good and marvelous in every situation.*

# JANUARY 22

*"People are at their most mindful when they are at play.
If we find ways of enjoying our work, blurring the lines
between work and play, the gains will be greater."*

— Ellen Langer

If you've ever watched young children play, you know how
fully immersed they are in the reality they've created. Their
imaginations are turned on. They're completely engaged. They're
often connecting with other children. And they're happy.

What grown-up play activities create a similar experience for you?
What fires up your imagination? What engages you so completely
that you lose track of time and maybe even forget to check your
phone? What makes you happy while you're doing it?

Play is mindfulness in motion. And if you and your colleagues
can develop ways to make your work together more playful,
so much the better.

*When I play, I am mindful. I will try to be more
playful in everything I do.*

# JANUARY 23

*"Have a mind that is open to everything and attached to nothing."*
— Tilopa

The Buddhist philosophy of unattachment means avoiding overdependence on certain outcomes or results. If we expect that if we do A then B will follow…but then B doesn't follow and we are upset by that, we were overly attached to the expected outcome. This leads to disappoint, a victim mentality, and mindless living.

I'll be honest with you. The mindfulness principle of unattachment to outcome has been a challenging one for me. I grew up believing that if I worked hard, I would achieve certain things, for example. And through nose-to-the-grindstone effort and daily control, many of those expectations have indeed worked out for me. But I slowly learned, over the course of decades, to relax and not be so worried about outcome. "Do good things and good things will follow" is now my mantra.

I'm open to what this day brings. I begin it with a clear intention about how I want to engage with the world, but I also try to accept and trust whatever happens.

*I am open to everything and accept whatever happens.*

# JANUARY 24

*"A great deal of the chaos in the world occurs because
people don't appreciate themselves."*

— Chogyam Trungpa

As we work through this book together, we're searching, at least
in part, for peace. We're on a day-by-day quest to live every
moment from a place of awareness, equanimity, and intention.

Chaos is the opposite of what we seek. We can't control the
chaos around us, but we are working on taming the chaos
within. And the chaos within is caused by our own responses,
which are our choice.

When we choose to doubt ourselves, be ashamed of ourselves,
treat ourselves unkindly, or judge ourselves harshly in any
way, we are stirring the maelstrom of internal chaos. If we
seek always to treat ourselves with compassion, kindness,
and gratitude, on the other hand, we are choosing to calm the
waters. And our internal placidness will in turn influence others
and foster mindfulness among those around us.

As within, so without.

*I appreciate myself. I treat myself with compassion,
kindness, and gratitude.*

# JANUARY 25

*"People who don't take risks generally make about two big mistakes a year. People who do take risks generally make about two big mistakes a year."*

— Peter F. Drucker

I'm a big believer in risk-taking. Life is short, and if you don't ever put yourself on the line, you'll end up on your deathbed regretting all the things you yearned to do but never even tried.

But what does this philosophy have to do with mindfulness, you ask? If I'm living in the now, you say, I'm not making big plans for the future. Instead, I'm staying present in *this* moment.

You've got a valid point. But here's the thing: Our creative impulses and grand dreams also arise and grow stronger in the present moment. We often can't bring them to fruition in an hour or a day, but we can live in the now with them by daydreaming, researching, putting notes on paper, and committing to next steps. And if we're true and diligent, we'll eventually have to take some kind of a risk to see the project to completion. That too, I believe, is an essential part of mindful living.

Sometimes our souls have big plans that only incremental mindfulness and courage can achieve.

*I will take risks to reach for my dreams.*

# JANUARY 26

*"I want Death to find me planting my cabbages."*
— Michel De Montaigne

If you could choose, what would you do on the day you die?
Just as an exercise, let's imagine this for a moment. Picture
yourself on a morning in the future. You are still as physically
well as you are today. You become aware that when the
sun sets on that day, you will die.

So what would you do with your one precious day? I think
I would say some "I love yous." I would hold some hands. I
would go for a hike and appreciate our earth. I might cry a little,
because I love this life and transitions hurt. And I'd gather my
family to sit on the deck with me and watch the sun go down.

Whatever we'd do on our final day, we should mindfully do
more of it on this—and every—day.

*Imagining what I would like to be doing on the day
I die helps me live this day better.*

# JANUARY 27

*"Each day means a new twenty-four hours. Each day means everything's possible again. You live in the moment; you die in the moment; you take it all one day at a time."*

— Marie Lu

Thinking of each new day as a clean slate can help us live mindfully. If we're not regretting yesterday and we're not worrying about tomorrow, we're living in the here and now.

It's kind of like putting blinders on a horse. Blinders help the animal to stay focused on the road right in front of him and not get distracted or upset by all the craziness going on in the periphery.

I think I'll consider every new day a mini-life. Wow! What an opportunity! What can I do today—just this one day—to live with intention, connection, and joy?

*This day, everything is possible.*

# JANUARY 28

*"If you give yourself one complete minute of focused presence, to simply stop, even to listen to your heart beating, it will take you out of your head and introduce you to the moment…which is complete in itself. It is not on the way to another moment. It is not a bridge to another opportunity. It is the timeless perfection. So stop…and sink into this timeless moment."*

— Mooji

This book is set up with a one-day-a-time mentality. If we can learn to better live one day at a time, we'll be making strides toward mindfulness. That's true.

But what's even truer is that the now unfolds not one *day* at a time but one *moment* at a time. And we've lived quite a few moments just since you started reading this page!

Whenever we're frantic or anxious, we can remember the power of the moment. We can stop whatever we're doing, close our eyes, and simply exist. We can luxuriate in simply breathing and being here on this amazing planet. We can stop…and sink into the timeless perfection of this moment.

*Each day, I will give myself at least one minute of focused presence.*

# JANUARY 29

*"Fear is a natural reaction to moving closer to the truth."*
— Pema Chödrön

Fear can be a big baby, I've noticed. Unless we're in immediate physical danger (in which case fear is essential, and we should take it seriously!), fear is often cowardly. It keeps us from straying outside our comfort zones. When we're trying to live mindfully, fear encourages us to look away from hard truths even though what we're actually trying to do is understand them.

In the quote above, teacher and Buddhist nun Pema Chödrön is recommending that we see our fear as a sign of progress. If we're working on mindfulness and we feel a bit uncomfortable or afraid, that means we're probably on the right track.

Awareness and presence can lead us to spotlight and question all kinds of assumptions about our lives. We might find ourselves wondering if we're in the right relationship or the right city. We might discover long-buried griefs or desires, and attending to them will require us to shake things up. In these cases, it's natural to feel afraid, but it also means we're homing in on essential truths.

*When I'm afraid, it's OK. It just means*
*I'm moving closer to the truth.*

# JANUARY 30

*"No, I never saw an angel, but it is irrelevant whether I saw
one or not. I feel their presence around me."*

— Paulo Coelho

Do you ever get the feeling that there's more to this world than
what we can experience with our five senses? I don't know
about you, but I'm open to the mystery. I've worked with
grieving people for more than forty years, and hundreds of them
have related stories of various sorts of encounters they've had
with loved ones who have died.

When we are living in the now, we are more intuitive. We're
paying more attention to the feedback from our five senses,
but we're also more attuned to other subtleties, such as odd
coincidences, gut feelings, and "vibes."

Maybe there are angels all around us. Many people believe there
are. Living with presence may help you feel *their* presence.

*I am open to the mysteries of the intangible.*

# JANUARY 31

*"At its deepest levels, life is not a problem but a mystery.*
*The distinction is fundamental: problems are to be solved; true*
*mysteries are not. And what does mystery ask of us? Only that we*
*be in its presence, that we fully, consciously hand ourselves over.*
*That is all, and that is everything."*

— Phil Simmons

The big questions of life and death are mysteries, I agree. Why do
we live? Why do we die? What's the purpose of human life? Why
do good people suffer? What happens after death? What will
happen to the human race 100 or 500 or 1,000 years from now?

It's interesting to ponder such mysteries, but for most
of us, it's counterproductive to try to solve them.
We can use up our lives stressing over and debating
these and other existential conundrums.

Some contemporary philosophers believe that the purpose of
biological life is for the universe to have a way to experience
itself. That's pretty esoteric, but what it essentially means is
that we've been put here to enjoy life. We're supposed to live
and love deeply. We're supposed to spend time in nature and
appreciate beauty. We're supposed to relish everything the
earth and human existence have to offer. In short, we're
supposed to live—ta-da!—in the now.

*I was born to relish everything the earth and human existence*
*have to offer. I was born to live in the now.*

# FEBRUARY 1

*"I have been impressed with the urgency of doing. Knowing is not enough; we must apply. Being willing is not enough; we must do."*

— Leonardo da Vinci

Life is short, my friends.

When we bring the power of mindfulness and intention to our goals and dreams, we give them momentum. We gather the energy to move closer to them. Simply daydreaming, on the other hand, or wishing and hoping, often get us nowhere.

Daydreaming, wishing, and hoping are all creative precursor activities. They help us imagine and clarify our possibilities. Mindful intentionality comes next. We know what we want, and we're setting out to get it. We're ready to *do*.

So let's go mindfully *do* something that feels essential today. Let's act with the urgency required of our short lives here on earth.

---

*Thinking is not enough. I must also do.*

# FEBRUARY 2

*"I engaged in the world. And I think there is great joy in being awake, alert, and alive to where we are."*

— Terry Tempest Williams

When we're awake to our lives, we're paying attention. We're noticing.

We're also alive to where and when and why we are. We're not just shuffling numbly through our days. Instead, we're charged with the energy of awareness and openness to experience.

Wake up! Notice your surroundings. Look away from your electronics. Gaze into the eyes of the people you care about. Strive to be alert and alive. Relish all the many joys of this day.

*I find joy in being awake, alert, and alive to where I am.*

# FEBRUARY 3

*"Humility does not mean believing oneself to be inferior but to be freed from self-importance. It is a state of natural simplicity that is in harmony with our true nature and allows us to taste the freshness of the present moment."*

— Matthieu Ricard

When I enter a situation or moment with humility, I come to it with a beginner's mind. I welcome whatever may happen. I try not to judge or stress or preplan or control. I flow into the moment, and I allow the moment to teach me.

Mostly, humility requires subduing our egos. That's a really hard part of our mindfulness practice. Our egos are divas, and they don't like playing second fiddle.

But when we achieve humility, we are open and receptive. We are more capable of an authentic encounter with the now. Yes, let's taste the freshness of the present moment.

*I enter the present moment with humility.*

# FEBRUARY 4

*"There is no safe investment. To love at all is to be vulnerable."*

— C.S. Lewis

Truer words were never spoken.

Love and grief are opposite sides of the same precious coin.
They are the yin and yang of our lives. When we open ourselves
to love, we open ourselves to pain. That's the deal.

Love is why we're here. It's our *raison d'etre*, or reason
for being. But when we lose something or someone we love,
it hurts above all else.

Love is not safe. But it's still the best investment there is.
So today, I hope we'll remember to put it all on the line for love.

*I will put it all on the line for love.*

# FEBRUARY 5

*"On days when the sky is gray, the sun has not disappeared forever."*
— Arnaud Desjardins

Life is fleeting, and so are many of our troubles.

When it comes to the hard parts in life—such as spats
with loved ones, financial problems, job issues, life partner
challenges, the death of someone we care about—mindfulness
can be especially challenging. It calls for us to stay present to
our naturally hurtful thoughts and feelings.
Instead of distracting ourselves, we must bear witness
to the truth of our pain.

But even as we are appropriately wallowing in the hurt,
we must also choose to hold onto hope.
Hope is an expectation of a good that is yet to be.

Hope is the knowing that the sun has not disappeared
forever. So we live in the gray now, but we trust that
the clouds will break.

*Even on days when the sky is gray, I will remember
that the sun has not disappeared forever.*

# FEBRUARY 6

*"There are as many atoms in a single molecule of your DNA as there are stars in a typical galaxy. We are, each of us, a little universe."*

— Neil Degrasse Tyson

Please indulge me while I get science-y for a minute.

An uncoiled human DNA molecule is a whisper-thin thread. It's about two inches long and contains about 204 billion atoms. And with new electron microscopes, we can see those individual atoms! High-power telescopes are allowing us to see more and more galactic wonders as well.

Yet we're really just beginning to understand space, time, the brain, and consciousness. Both the universe and the human body are mysterious and amazing.

You are here. I am here. What a privilege that we get to be here. What a privilege that we get to be here together.

*Inside me and outside me are miracles.*
*It is a privilege to be here.*

# FEBRUARY 7

*"Don't ask what the world needs.*
*Ask what makes you come alive, and go do it.*
*Because what the world needs is people who have come alive."*

— Howard Thurman

Sometimes when I read the news or catch the headlines on TV, I'm struck with despair. So many terrible things happen every day. I want to help, but how? In the face of these problems, I am an insignificant, powerless speck.

Yet when I remember that I have the power to touch those around me, I get reenergized. I still myself and listen to my inner voice. It tells me what's truly important to me. It reminds me what I'm passionate about. Then, when I mindfully act on those passions, I create connections in the world. I make a difference in my life but also the lives of others, and those people affect more people, and so on and so on and so on. If everyone acted from this egoless place of truth and light, hate, violence, poverty, and hunger would be eradicated in no time.

What makes you come alive? Go do that.

*I am mindfully working to understand what*
*makes me come alive so I can go do it.*

# FEBRUARY 8

*"After all the years of [spiritual] work, I've realized this: that everything and everyone is precious beyond words. Everything and everyone is holy. And the point of our being on this sweet planet is to be of service to all of it. And when we understand this truth in our bones, joy fills our hearts."*

— Geri Larkin

You know that feeling you get sometimes when your child blows out the birthday candles or you unexpectedly do something kind for someone else or you have the rare opportunity to take a walk on the beach hand-in-hand with your beloved? That feeling of overwhelming gratitude just to be here on this earth—and you can't speak because no words are adequate?

Turns out that everything in the world is just as miraculous. When we learn to live mindfully, we get better and better at seeing that. This random mug on my desk is a wonder. This computer I'm typing on—holy cow. And the view out my writing hut's window? It's so beautiful I can, if I'm living in the now, be moved to tears.

So first I work on the noticing and appreciating. Then I work on the doing—the participating in ways that serve humanity and this sweet planet.

*I am working on the noticing, appreciating, participating, and serving.*

# FEBRUARY 9

*"Between stimulus and response there is a space.*
*In that space is our power to choose our response.*
*In our response lies our growth and our freedom."*

— Victor Frankl

In part, mindfulness is about training ourselves to recognize that space between stimulus and response. Let's say someone cuts us off in traffic. What do we do? Do we immediately honk or yell or gesture in anger at the other driver? Or do we instead pause for a breath and choose our response mindfully?

The point is, we are in control of our own actions. If our intention is to foster kindness and compassion in the world, for example, through mindfulness we can learn to recognize which situations tend to trigger us into actions that are less than kind and compassionate. We can teach ourselves to experience the stimulus, bear witness to our internal feelings of anger or blame or fear, and then respond with calm kindness.

Experience, feel, pause to acknowledge the feeling and craft a response that is in keeping with our intentions, then respond. In that tiny gap between experience and response lives a world of new possibilities.

*In the gap between a stimulus and my response*
*lies my growth and freedom.*

# FEBRUARY 10

*"Efficiency is doing things right.*
*Effectiveness is doing the right things."*
— Peter Drucker

I do a lot of speaking about grief and healing to groups around the world, and one central principle I often teach audiences is that of efficiency versus effectiveness.

When we are being efficient, we are getting things done quickly but often mindlessly. We are focused on checking tasks off our to-do lists. When we are being effective, on the other hand, we are first pausing to reflect on the goal of what we are doing. We are shining the flashlight of our awareness on the task at hand, and we are seeking to complete the task (if we decide it needs to be completed at all) in a manner that best fulfills the task's deepest purposes, which always come down to experiencing, expressing, and connecting. We are also remaining mindful throughout.

Today, in all we do, let's choose effectiveness over efficiency. Mindfulness may not always be efficient, but it is always effective.

*I choose effectiveness over efficiency.*

# FEBRUARY 11

*"The discipline involved in finishing a piece of creative work is some-
thing on which you can truly pride yourself. You'll have turned from
somebody who's 'thinking of,' 'who might,' 'who's trying to,'
to someone who DID. And once you've done it,
you know you can do it again."*

— J.K. Rowling

I'm definitely a believer in Big Hairy Audacious Goals, or
BHAGs. Coined by leadership guru and author Jim Collins
about 25 years ago, the term means a goal that's visionary—
really big and bold. In their time, mass producing the
automobile and putting a man on the moon were BHAGs.

Individual people have BHAGs too. In my life so far,
mine have included earning my Ph.D., writing books,
and starting the Center for Loss.

The question is, what are *your* unfinished BHAGs? It's not too
late to get started on them. Pick one and take a step toward
it today, then another step tomorrow. If you need help with
discipline or learning the how-tos, find a mentor, take lessons,
or work with a life coach. You've got this.

*I'm working on a BHAG. Today's step is*

_____.

# FEBRUARY 12

*"Living 24 hours with mindfulness is more worthwhile*
*than living 100 years without it."*

— Buddha

At first, practicing mindfulness can be exhausting. We're so used to whizzing through our days in a constant stream of mindless busyness and doing and technology and entertainment that when we slow down and really experience each moment, we get burned out. It's a little like having an intense, life-changing conversation with someone we care about—we know it's important, but it's draining. We couldn't do it 24/7.

To counteract this natural fatigue, it's OK to allow yourself periods of mindless TV or internet surfing or whatever relaxes you in between your mindful blocks of time. As with weightlifting or meditation, the more you practice mindfulness, the more you'll be able to handle.

Eventually you'll find that living mindfully is so transformative, mindless living is lackluster in comparison.

*I am working on living with mindfulness*
*more and more each day.*

# FEBRUARY 13

*"Respond to every call that excites your spirit."*

— Rumi

Have you ever stumbled across something on Facebook or walked by a certain place or happened upon a random conversation that made your heart beat a little faster and your mind say, "Hey! I love this!"

I believe our spirits know why we're here on earth. We came here with a purpose (or maybe several purposes) to fulfill, but many of us forget or get sidetracked along the way. Through mindfulness, we can reconnect with our reason for being, or *raison d'etre*, as the French say.

All we have to do is notice what excites our spirit then pursue it. If we train our awareness on the amplitude of our divine spark—what makes it grow stronger, what weakens it—we'll start living more authentically. Let's heed our call.

*I will respond to every call that excites my spirit.*

# FEBRUARY 14

*"I have never met a person whose greatest need was
anything other than real, unconditional love."*

— Elisabeth Kübler-Ross

If the Beatles are to be believed, all we need is love. They're
right, of course. You can strip everything else away from us,
but if you leave us the people we care about, we'll collapse in a
puddle of relief and gratitude.

When we have love in our lives, we must work each and every
day to mindfully acknowledge it for what it is: a privilege. It's all
too easy to start taking it for granted. Mindfulness helps us stay
aware of the miracle of another person's affection and presence.

It's Valentine's Day. Today's the day to let the people we care
about know that we care about them. Big gestures aren't
necessary. Let's go for heartfelt, mindful clarity instead—
perhaps a personalized, handwritten note to each of the
people we couldn't live without.

*Mindfulness helps me stay aware of the
miracle of love in my life.*

# FEBRUARY 15

*"If you concentrate on finding whatever is good in every situation,
you will discover that your life will suddenly be filled with gratitude,
a feeling that nurtures the soul."*

— Rabbi Harold Kushner

When we're feeling bad about insignificant worries, we can choose to look for the good.

I don't know about you, but I can be irritable. Irritability is generally mindless. But when I stop and catch myself in a state of irritation, I can mindfully choose to consider the source of my feelings. Often it's just my ego getting annoyed or anxious over something trivial or outside my control.

Then I look for the good. What do I have to be grateful for on this day? What surrounds me that is miraculous and noteworthy, if I only give it the attention it deserves? What special people can I spend time or connect with during this day? Gratitude is simply mindfulness of what is good.

*When I find the good in every situation,
I am filled with gratitude.*

# FEBRUARY 16

*"You and I appear to be separate. We differ in color, size, and shape…in ideas, tastes, and prejudices. Beneath this apparent division, however, hidden deep within each of us, is the one Self—eternal, infinite, ever-perfect. This is the closely guarded secret of life: that we are all caught up in a divine masquerade, and all we are trying to do is take off our masks to reveal the pure, perfect Self within."*

— Eknath Easwaran

We are not bodies with souls. We are souls embodied. And our bodies come in all sizes, shapes, and colors. They're also born into a certain time, place, and culture.

But all those particulars are not who we are. Our souls are who we are. And each person's soul is precious and divine. What's more, all souls are part of the same, unified divinity. It is only because of our mindless egos that we learn to believe the lie that we are different and separate from one another.

Mindfulness is about unmasking ourselves and each other to allow the souls within to shine forth. *Namaste* is a Buddhist greeting that means "the divine in me recognizes and honors the divine in you." Namaste.

*The divine in me recognizes and honors the divine in you.*

# FEBRUARY 17

*"Our challenge each day is not to get dressed to face the world but to unglove ourselves so that the doorknob feels cold and the car handle feels wet and the kiss goodbye feels like the lips of another being, soft and unrepeatable."*

— Mark Nepo

Have you ever noticed that we tend to shield ourselves from each other and from life?

The following apply to many but not all of us:

We dress in certain ways so that we blend in. We look past strangers instead of at them. We prefer texting over phone calls. We shy away from joining, leading, risking, feeling.

But what if the whole point of human life is to follow our whims, stand out, connect, join, lead, risk, and feel?
I think it is, actually.

So today, let's remember to unglove ourselves.

.

*I will unglove myself.*

# FEBRUARY 18

*"We must be willing to let go of the life we have planned so as to have the one that is waiting for us."*

— E.M. Forster

Sometimes mindfulness reconciles us to a different path than the one we had hoped to take.

I advocate for using mindfulness to pursue our passions and dreams. Intentional, mindful perseverance is a powerful force. But still, it's true that we can't always get what we want. Because life happens. We lose a job or we get injured or someone who's a part of us dies.

What do we do then? We intentionally, mindfully mourn. We acknowledge and express our grief for as long as we need to. We mourn our loss honestly, and over time we learn to embrace our new, changed life. We stay present, aware, and hopeful about whatever's around the next corner. We work to live in mindfulness throughout.

*Whenever life takes me in a different direction than the one I had planned, I will mourn and live fully in my new present.*

# FEBRUARY 19

*"Daring greatly means the courage to be vulnerable. It means to show up and be seen. To ask for what you need. To talk about how you're feeling. To have the hard conversations."*

— Dr. Brené Brown

Mindfulness is awareness of what is going on both inside and outside of you. It's paying attention. It's noticing.
But *acting* mindfully, on the other hand, is about taking the awareness you have gained through mindfulness and choosing what to *do* with it in the world.

Acting mindfully is expressing the realizations of your mindfulness. It's speaking your truth. It's showing up and stating your intention.

Acting mindfully takes daring. So few people act mindfully that when we see it, we sometimes mistake it for brashness or confrontation. But it's not—it's simply the clarity of mindfulness taking action in the world. And since true mindfulness is never selfish or mean-spirited, its intention is always honorable.

So *be* mindful then *act* mindfully. Dare yourself to go for it.

*I will be mindful then act mindfully. I must do both.*

# FEBRUARY 20

*"God made the world round so we would never be able
to see too far down the road."*

— Isak Dinesen

We don't get to see our futures. Thank goodness. Can you
imagine how much joy would be sucked out of the special
moments in our futures if we knew of them in advance? It'd
be like opening a life's worth of birthday presents and scrolling
through a life's worth of photos all at once.

And can you further imagine how much more terrible it
would be to know when and how troubles would be headed
our way? No thanks.

Life's uncertainty is what makes it interesting. It also allows us
to nurture hope, which is an expectation of a good that is yet to
be. Without hope, prospects are grim.

Plan for and be hopeful about the future, yes, but live for today.
Right now, this spot in the road we're standing on is everything.

*I look to the horizon but I live today.*

# FEBRUARY 21

*"You do not belong to you. You belong to the universe. The significance of you will forever remain obscure to you, but you may assume that you are fulfilling your significance if you apply yourself to converting all your experience to the highest advantage of others."*

— Buckminster Fuller

Some days mindfulness seems impossible. When we're too busy and having to multitask our way through the day, or when we're really stressed out about a challenging situation in our life, remaining centered and present feels like a lost cause.

But on these days, what if we remind ourselves that our purpose is higher than whatever's on our plate at the moment? I sometimes picture myself floating up and away from Earth, out of the solar system, past the Milky Way galaxy, past the Virgo Supercluster, and out into the billions of galaxies beyond. How's that for perspective?

And what if on our most mindless days (for it's impossible to avoid them completely) we strive to apply every action we take to the highest advantage of others? In other words, what if we try to be conscious of the most fundamental *why* of what we are doing in each moment?

*I belong to the universe. I am fulfilling my significance by applying myself to help others.*

# FEBRUARY 22

*"First I was dying to finish high school and start college.
And then I was dying to finish college and start working.
And then I was dying to marry and have children.
And then I was dying for my children to grow old enough for
school so I could return to work. And then I was dying to retire.
And now, I am dying...and suddenly realizing I forgot to live."*

— Author Unknown

Planning ahead and forgoing small gratifications today to
achieve large gratifications in the future are worthy pursuits.
I believe our souls yearn for meaning and purpose, which are
often incrementally realized over the long-term.

Yet planning for the future doesn't mean we can't be mindfully
present and appreciative of today. It's not an either/or
proposition! In fact, like all the best and truest things
in life, it's an "and" proposition.

If you have babies still in diapers, for instance, you can both
relish their fleeting babyhood *and* look forward to the day when
they're potty trained. If you're training to compete in your first
marathon, you can mindfully stay present to this day's training
run *and* envision crossing the finish line a few months hence.

I hasten to add, however, that your life is now. While it's wise
and even mindful to devote a portion of today to tomorrow,
most of today is for today. Live it well.

*Planning is good, but most of today is for today. I will live it well.*

# FEBRUARY 23

*"Leave your front door and your back door open.*
*Allow your thoughts to come and go. Just don't serve them tea."*
— Shunryu Suzuki

Our minds, in service of our egos, like to take over.
They're prone to fretting and flying off in all different directions.
They want to control things, so they trick us into
believing they're Important Thoughts.

In today's reflection, Zen monk and teacher Shunryu Suzuki
reminds us that our thoughts are just passing fancies.
We must notice them then let them move on. Whatever we do,
we shouldn't hold tight to them and revere them as if they
were gospel. We shouldn't serve them tea.

It's interesting that mindfulness requires getting out of our heads
and stepping into the true inner sanctums of our souls. In this
way, mindfulness is not about what we often think of as the
mind. Instead, it is a more spiritual capacity for getting in
touch with the infinite Truth.

*I mindfully observe my thoughts flowing through me.*

# FEBRUARY 24

*"Every morning I awake torn between a desire to
save the world and an inclination to savor it.
This makes it hard to plan the day.
But if we forget to savor the world,
what possible reason do we have for saving it?
In a way, the savoring must come first."*

— E.B. White

Those of you reading this who are, like me, natural caregivers
will appreciate today's reminder.

Our awareness reveals the world around us.
Mindfulness shows us the good, the bad, and everything
in between. The challenge is, we often feel compelled to fix the
bad. We want to help other people. We also may want to help
the environment, on which all people depend. But how can
we take care of others and the earth while also staying present
and mindful in our own day-to-day lives?

I think it's a question of balance. When I'm grief counseling,
I'm mindfully present to the person I'm helping. When I'm not
working, I'm mindfully present to savoring my own existence.
For me, both are essential to nurturing my divine spark.

*I can both save and savor. It's a question of mindful balance.*

# FEBRUARY 25

*"If I were called upon to state in a few words the essence of everything
I was trying to say, it would be something like this: Listen to your life.
See it for the fathomless mystery that it is. In the boredom and pain of
it no less than in the excitement and gladness: touch, taste, smell your
way to the holy and hidden heart of it because in the last analysis all
moments are key moments, and life itself is grace."*

— Frederick Buechner

What's a miracle? Everything's a miracle.

The fact that you are alive is a miracle, and every moment of
your aliveness is a miracle. Are you bored? In pain? Excited?
Glad? Whatever you're feeling and experiencing, it's a miracle.

Albert Einsten famously said, "There are only two
ways to live your life. One is as though nothing is a miracle.
The other is as though everything is a miracle."
The latter, my friend, is the way to go.

*All moments are key moments, and life itself is grace.*

# FEBRUARY 26

*"Man should not try to avoid stress any more than he would shun food, love, or exercise."*

— Hans Selye

Hans Selye was a Hungarian physician and the father of research on stress's effects on the body. In fact, he coined the word "stress," in 1936. He determined that there is bad stress—which he called "distress"—and good stress—which he called "eustress" (*eu* meaning "good" or "well" in Greek).

We experience eustress when we move through growth-oriented life transitions, such as getting married, having a child, and buying a home. We experience distress when we divorce unwillingly, suffer physical problems, get laid off from a job we are attached to, or lose a loved one.

The thing is, we will naturally experience distress along life's path. We don't have to go looking for it. But if we are overly cautious and afraid to risk, we may miss out on eustress too. And that is tantamount to shunning love and joy. So let's mindfully pursue eustress. It's where all the best stuff can be found.

*Stress can be good. I seek out good stress.*

# FEBRUARY 27

*"Everywhere in nature we are taught the lessons of patience and waiting. We want things a long time before we get them, and the fact that we want them a long time makes them all the more precious when they come."*

— Joseph F. Smith

I have noticed that for many people, one of the hardest parts of mindful living is choosing, in the moment, between reveling in the now and delaying gratification for the sake of longer-term goals.

Let's say you're passionate about doing something that will take years or even decades to accomplish. Maybe you have a dream to save people's lives by becoming a transplant surgeon or simply live in a nice home that you will buy and maintain yourself. Achieving such goals take patience and hard work, and also, yes, sacrifices in the now.

If you have to study, you may not be able to hang out with your friends this afternoon. If you're saving money, you probably can't go to Starbucks today. But mindfully making these choices in the now and applying yourself today to the activities that will get you where you want to go in the future is mindfulness with a purpose. In fact, I believe it's just as essential as the "live it up today" sort of mindfulness.

The trick is to balance the two. Too much of the former and you run the risk of all work and no play. Too much of the latter and you may well end up feeling you've frittered your life away.

*I balance delayed gratification with daily gratification.*

# FEBRUARY 28

*"When we lose one we love, our bitterest tears are called forth
by the memory of hours when we loved not enough."*

— Maurice Maeterlinck

Yesterday we talked about mindfully delaying small gratifications in the now in order to achieve big dreams in the future. Today I'd like to talk about the mindful path of choosing people over productivity.

As you know, I'm a grief counselor who well understands the devastation people naturally experience when someone they love dies. They never regret time they spent with their loved one. They often regret time they spent on other things, like working too much or activities they didn't really care about.

But—and this is a big but—mourners usually see the value in reasonable amounts of time that they or the person who died spent pursuing true passions. Do you see the difference? The overall mindfulness takeaway is: Make time for people. Spend necessary time pursuing goals that give your life purpose. Choose not to waste time on meaningless activities.

*I make time both for people I care about and for
activities that give my life purpose.*

# MARCH 1

*"We can only be said to be alive in those moments when our hearts are conscious of our treasures."*

—Thornton Wilder

What do I value most?

If we live each day with the answer to this question first and foremost in our awareness, we can't help but be mindful. For one, trivialities fall away. As author Richard Carlson famously wrote, "Don't sweat the small stuff…and it's all small stuff." For another, we're more apt to spend our precious spare time on things that really matter.

My treasures are my family (including my dogs and my friends who are like family), the privilege I have to teach and converse with others about grief and healing, and nature. On days when I manage to keep my heart conscious of these, I feel more calm and contented, no matter how chaotic or mundane things get.

So I'll ask you: What do you value most?
Live today with your answer top of mind.

---

*Here's what I value most:*

_____.

# MARCH 2

*"Be yourself. Everyone else is already taken."*
— Oscar Wilde

As I travel the world to speak about the natural and necessary process of grief and healing, I meet a lot of people. On airplanes and in hotel lobbies and after my talks, I often end up chatting with strangers who tell me their unique stories.

And what I realize is that every story is a miracle. I'm constantly amazed by the singular beauty and heartache of each individual's life.

Whoever you are, you're a humdinger. I believe that, and you should believe that too. Besides, you can't mindfully live *your* life if you're not living your life, you know what I mean? Any falseness or insecurity you allow to linger will only diminish your capacity to live genuinely in the now.

Only the true you lives in the now.

*I can only mindfully live my life if I am living my life.*

# MARCH 3

*"The next message you need is always right where you are."*
— Ram Dass

This, I think, is an intriguing way to spend a day or a week or a month, just to see what happens. If you assume that the universe presents you with whatever you most need, when you need it, you can let go of worry. You can live in the moment and rest assured that all will be well.

Notice, though, that spiritual teacher Ram Dass isn't promising, for example, that money will magically appear when you're broke or that other people will do what you think they should do. Instead, he's saying that you can be sure the universe will always give you the *next* message you need to hear.

Let's say I'm worried about an issue I'm having with one of my children. I'm not sure what to do. Maybe if I still myself and practice living in the now, an answer will arise effortlessly. The answer may not solve the problem, but it will be the next idea or reassurance I need. It will be a breadcrumb on the trail. And I can trust that I'll also receive tomorrow's breadcrumb tomorrow.

*I receive the next message I need when I need it.*

# MARCH 4

*"For a seed to achieve its greatest expression, it must come completely undone. The shell cracks, its insides come out, and everything changes. To someone who doesn't understand growth, it would look like complete destruction."*

— Marcel Proust

As I shared with you in this book's introduction, I'm a grief and death professional. I know that significant loss or change of any kind—illness, divorce, job loss, relocation, the death of someone loved—causes us to grieve inside.

And grief, by its very nature, tears us apart.

You might have heard the word "bereaved" before. It's an old-fashioned term for someone who's grieving, and it literally means "to be torn apart." Grief destroys us, and we have to rebuild. Our new life will not be the same as our old life. It can still be good, maybe even better, but it will be different, and the scar and hurt of the old injury will always remain.

Mindfully experiencing loss requires staying present to the pain and honoring the changes it sets in motion. Sometimes living in the now is harder than at other times.

*Sometimes destruction precedes construction.*
*I will be mindful of this when I experience destruction.*

# MARCH 5

*"You live once and life is wonderful,*
*so eat the damned red velvet cupcake."*

— Emma Stone

What's your favorite indulgence? Mine is brownies.
I like nothing better than to eat three or four of them.
If I'm in a really hedonistic mood, I'll even put ice cream on
top. These are not things I do every day, because if I did, they
wouldn't be special anymore. But treating ourselves in simple
ways every day is an effective mindfulness tool.

Think about all the little things that give you a burst of pleasure,
such as enjoying a cup of your favorite tea, giving a loved one a
hug, singing along to your favorite song, or snuggling into the
heated seats in your car. If you consciously plan to sprinkle at
least four or five such mini-treats throughout your day,
you'll be helping yourself live in the now.

You live once and life is wonderful, so treat yourself,
every day (just not to three or four brownies!).

*I will only live once and life is wonderful,*
*so I will treat myself every day.*

# MARCH 6

*"Silence is not the absence of sound. It's a physical place,
a destination with value and meaning in a chaotic world, somewhere
arrived at with difficulty and left with regret."*

— Kenneth Turan

I have a home in the Arizona desert I often visit after a week of speaking and traveling across the country. I seek refuge there. Content in my aloneness, I settle in. I step outside to the patio and stretch myself out on the chaise longue. For an hour or two, I do not look at my phone. I do not open my laptop. I do not turn on the TV or listen to music. Instead, I retreat into the sanctuary of silence and simply breathe.

Silence is restorative, but if you're someone who's uncomfortable being alone or who likes to keep the TV on at all times just for the background noise, it can be a difficult practice to cultivate. I promise you, though—it's worth it. Learning to retreat into silence regularly will help you locate and nurture your divine spark.

Essentially, cultivating silence is the art of depriving yourself of outer experience for a time so that you can focus on your inner awareness. Once you have found it, you will be ready, sometimes regretfully, to return to the outer world, ready to mindfully experience and appreciate the now.

*In solitude and silence I can locate and nurture my divine spark.*

# MARCH 7

*"Remembering that you are going to die is the best way I know to avoid the trap of thinking you have something to lose. You are already naked. There is no reason not to follow your heart."*

— Steve Jobs

You know that thing you've been wanting to try but haven't? Really and truly, what have you got to lose?

If you try it, will you forever lose someone you care about? Will you endanger your life or someone else's? Will you risk or lose a lot more money than you can afford? If the answer to all three questions is no, then you've got no legitimate excuse. And if the answer to any of these questions is yes, then you need to talk over your decision with a levelheaded person you trust.

What if I told you you were going to die next month? Wouldn't you throw caution to the wind and give it a go today?

Try as you might to put up safety shields around your life, you're still vulnerable in all the ways that count. There is no reason not to follow your heart.

*I have nothing to lose.*
*There is no reason not to follow my heart.*

# MARCH 8

*"You'll seldom experience regret for anything that you've done. It is what you haven't done that will torment you. The message, therefore, is clear. Do it! Develop an appreciation for the present moment. Seize every second of your life and savor it. Value your present moments. Using them up in any self-defeating ways means you've lost them forever."*

— Wayne Dyer

Living in the now is about seizing every second. We're reminding ourselves of this fact 365 times in this book. Looking at the flip side can also be helpful. We're prone to wasting time too often, yes. But we also might be spending time defeating and harming ourselves.

Our divine sparks, evidenced by our feelings of interest and love, guide us in seizing seconds positively. Time-killing activities like mindlessly surfing the Web and binge-watching TV indicate when we're spending time in neutral. And harmful behaviors are red flags warning us that we're not just wasting precious years, we're at risk of a life tragically lived.

Addictions are an example of self-defeating behavior. Domestic violence, untreated mental or physical health problems, and legal troubles are others. If you're struggling with any harmful situation or behavior, I urge you to seek the assistance of a counselor, physician, or attorney. You won't be able to live mindfully until you mindfully reach out for help. If this applies to you, that is your mindfulness task for today— and every day until you're on a healthy path.

*If I am acting in self-defeating ways, it's time for me to seek help.*

# MARCH 9

*"The key to creating the mental space before responding is mindfulness. Mindfulness is a way of being present: paying attention to and accepting what is happening in our lives. It helps us to be aware of and step away from our automatic and habitual reactions to our everyday experiences."*

— Elizabeth Thornton

Some of our responses we can control; some we cannot.

When we notice a nearby object, such as a ball, flying toward us, we either duck out of the way to avoid it or we reach out to catch it. When we touch something hot, we pull our hand away. These are automatic reflexes. Our body takes control to protect us.

But many of our responses are not truly instinctive—they just seem that way. If I snap at my wife every time we're in a certain situation, that isn't "just the way I am." Instead, that is my choice. If I shine the light of awareness on my habitual response, I will see that the next time I find myself in this situation, I can create the mental space to consciously choose to respond differently.

Whatever bad habits we may have, we can use the power of mindfulness to change them. We need not judge or shame ourselves along the way. Humans are not perfect.
But what a glorious moment when we succeed in mindfully changing a behavior that has long plagued us.

*I can change my habitual reactions if I approach them mindfully.*

# MARCH 10

*"We spend precious hours fearing the inevitable.
It would be wise to use that time adoring our families,
cherishing our friends, and living our lives."*

— Maya Angelou

Fear may be normal, but it's a time-waster.

Often, being afraid is borrowing trouble. We're apprehensive about something that *might* happen tomorrow, so we spend time worrying about it today. Both today and tomorrow are squandered. And what if the worried-about happening doesn't materialize? Then we've really wasted precious hours.

Of course, sometimes, as Maya Angelou notes,
we fear things that do in fact come to pass.
The expected layoff happens. Our children leave the nest.
Someone we love who is terminally ill dies.

It's normal to fear inevitable loss, but mindfulness can help us redirect our fear, which is making our bodies and our hearts sick. We can choose to focus instead on adoring our families, cherishing our friends, and living our nows.

*I am mindful not to waste precious hours fearing the
inevitable. Instead, I use that time to adore my family,
cherish my friends, and live my life.*

# MARCH 11

*"And remember, no matter where you go, there you are."*
— Confucius

We can't run away from ourselves. We try, though.
We overbook. We distract ourselves with all manner of inane
entertainment. (YouTube videos, anyone?) We indulge in
addictive behaviors.

Practicing mindfulness reacquaints us with ourselves. We
not only pay attention to what's going on around us, we pay
attention to what's going on inside us. We notice and experience
our feelings. We notice and experience our thoughts. We notice
and experience our responses to what's going on around us.

In befriending our true selves, we practice what meditation
teacher Tara Brach calls "radical self-acceptance." We get to
know ourselves, and we learn to be kind to ourselves. We
relinquish shame. We accept our own imperfections. We
embrace our own worthiness.

"Well hello, you," we say to ourselves. "There you are."

*I am mindfully befriending my true self.*

# MARCH 12

*"We each need to make our lion's roar—to persevere with unshakable courage when faced with all manner of doubts and sorrows and fears—to declare our right to awaken."*

— Jack Kornfield

I love this image of the roaring lion, and I agree that each of us has a roar inside us.

What's your roar? It's whatever you feel passionate about deep down—so passionate that if it were about to be taken away from you, you would roar instead of cowering in fear. This world needs more roaring.

Keep in mind, though, that a roar isn't an ignorant complaint, petty annoyance, or ego-based cry of injustice. It's more important than that. It's more eternal and divine. We shouldn't roar when someone takes our parking spot; we should roar when we witness mistreatment or have an idea to help solve a problem in our community.

We roar when we awaken to meaning and purpose.
Be a lion today.

*I will be a lion today.*

# MARCH 13

*"'The story of my recent life.' I like that phrase. It makes more sense than 'the story of my life,' because we get so many lives between birth and death. A life to be a child. A life to come of age. A life to wander, to settle, to fall in love, to parent, to test our promise, to realize our mortality—and in some lucky cases, to do something after that realization."*

— Mitch Albom

Life is chockfull of huge transitions. We're born, we're children, we're students. We begin a career. We marry. We relocate. We have children of our own. We raise children. We wave children goodbye. Friends come and go. Partners come and go. Jobs come and go. Change after major change after major change.

Each new phase of our lives is like a mini-life with its own story. What's the story of your recent life?

When we befriend our own mortality, our life story is enhanced from there forward. It's more colorful and richer and more meaningful. Staying mindful of our eventual death makes our living more urgent and purposeful. It gives each mini-life we have left to us a desirable poignancy. Lucky us.

*I am realizing my own mortality so that I can deeply live.*

# MARCH 14

*"If you clean the floor with love, you have given
the world an invisible painting."*

— Osho

If we apply mindfulness to the small, necessary tasks of our
days, we transform them into works of love.

If we load the dishwasher mindfully, we pay attention to
the aligning of cups and silverware, and we marvel at the
technology that will render them sparkling clean. We might also
give thanks for the food that nurtured us and our loved ones.

It's hard, though, isn't it? It's challenging to stay present to
seemingly mundane things we have to do almost every day,
especially if they're activities we don't enjoy. The trick is to
approach them with gratitude. "I'm grateful to have this safe,
cozy bed to sleep in every night" as we make the bed.
"I'm grateful for the abundance of food and goods my family
needs" as we collect the trash.

Actually, gratitude and love (the verb) make everything mindful.
As Mother Teresa said, we needn't worry about doing great
things. We only need to do small things with great love.

*Mindful gratitude and love make even small things meaningful.*

# MARCH 15

*"F-E-A-R has two meanings: Forget Everything And Run, or Face Everything And Rise. The choice is yours."*

— Zig Ziglar

I've met a lot of people who are afraid to really live. If you engage them in conversation, you'll discover that they have yearnings and flights of fancy, but they're not acting on them because they don't want to risk failure or ridicule. They're also likely to be harboring unexpressed feelings of anger, sadness, guilt, or shame, because these emotions also feel risky and over-challenging.

These are the people who Forget Everything And Run. They forget their passions and their hurts, and they run or hide from them, hoping they can escape. They can't.

Mindful people, on the other hand, Face Everything and Rise. You strive to look the truth in the face each day. You live vulnerably and fully. You experience everything. And in living with this kind of courage, you rise. Your awareness leads you to your best possible life. You've chosen well.

---

*At every crossroads, I choose to Face Everything And Rise.*

# MARCH 16

*"Our lives are lived in intense and anxious struggle,
in a swirl of speed and aggression, in competing, grasping,
possessing, and achieving, forever burdening ourselves
with extraneous activities and preoccupations."*

— Sogyal Rinpoche

I confess, in trying to balance my life between doing
and being, I too often tip toward doing.

By now you know that I'm a *carpe diem* kind of guy. I'm a
strong believer in the importance of taking risks, working
hard, and pursuing big goals. For me, the challenge comes
in remembering to allow plenty of time for downshifting into
neutral. For you, maybe the opposite is more of a challenge.

Life may be short, but it isn't a race. Nor is it a shoebox we
should try to jam-pack. So let's go slowly and mindfully about
our day, and let's not forget to build in ample time to simply be.

*My life today can be speedy and anxious,
or slow and calm. It's up to me.*

# MARCH 17

*"Remember that sometimes not getting what you
want is a wonderful stroke of luck."*

— Dalai Lama

In the now, we feel yearnings.
We want all kinds of things, big and little.

Throughout this book I encourage you to go after what you
want. Your divine spark whispers to you about your passions
and purposes, and then it's up to you to make them happen.
Sometimes, though, you don't get what you want, no matter
how hard you try. Sometimes life disappoints or even
seems to deliver the opposite.

How do you mindfully deal with disappointment? By embracing
it in the moment. By acknowledging and encountering it. And
by intentionally choosing what, if anything, to do about it.
Maybe it's lucky you didn't get what you wanted because what
you thought you wanted was actually all about ego. Or maybe
it's lucky because something better is around the corner. Or
perhaps you just need to buckle down and try again—and the
learning of perseverance is your lucky lesson for today.

*Sometimes I am lucky not to get what I want.*

# MARCH 18

*"Words may be false and full of art.*
*Sighs are the natural language of the heart."*

— Thomas Shadwell

We should pay attention to our sighs. For something so mindless, they're pretty smart.

When we feel annoyed, we might sigh with frustration. When we're delighted, we might sigh with pleasure. When we're exhausted, we might sigh with fatigue. We use sighs as a shorthand to express what we're feeling inside. And what we're feeling inside is the truth of our now.

If you catch yourself sighing today, ask yourself why. Mindfully consider what needs your sigh might be revealing. Do you need to rest? Do you need to take a break from what you're doing? Do you need to express feelings of love and connection to someone else? Sigh, reflect, act.

*When I catch myself sighing, I will mindfully ask why.*

# MARCH 19

*"You are only young once, but you can stay immature indefinitely."*
— Ogden Nash

Generally, young people are better at living in the now than grown-ups. Children, especially, live in the moment. They don't worry or plan ahead. They don't get caught in the flypaper of regretted yesterdays. Instead, they relish this minute, then the next minute, then the next.

But young people often aren't so good at delaying gratification or devoting hard work now in exchange for rewards down the line. And they haven't learned as much as older people, so they're more prone to make mistakes—sometimes large, life-altering ones.

What if we could mix the joie de vivre of youth with the wisdom of older age? I think we can. Our daily practice of living in the now helps with the former, and applying intention and mindfulness to our decision-making reinforces the latter. We *can* have it both ways—even if we can't do a handspring anymore.

*In mindfully mixing merriment and maturity,
I will find my sweet spot.*

# MARCH 20

*"There is no royal, flower-strewn path to success. And if there is,*
*I have not found it. For if I have accomplished anything in life,*
*it is because I have been willing to work hard."*

— C.J. Walker

My father was a worker. His strong German heritage
gave him a work ethic that bordered on workaholism.
From him I learned that if you put your nose to the grindstone,
you stand a pretty good chance of accomplishing
whatever you want to accomplish.

Hard work is a form of mindfulness. If you're focused on a task
and you see it through to completion, you are living in the now
of your effort. Ideally your work is your calling—something that
overlaps with your passions—because then you're
mindfully spending time on activities that have meaning
for you beyond a paycheck.

I hope you work hard and mindfully, but I also hope you're
balancing your work life with your personal life. My dad
didn't do that so well. I learned my work ethic from him, but
in bearing witness to his life I also learned the importance of
finding a better balance. Life is best with both.

*I work hard, but work is only a part of my life.*

# MARCH 21

*"Life is a process of becoming, a combination of states we have to go through. Where people fail is that they wish to elect a state and remain in it. This is a kind of death."*

— Anaïs Nin

There are two basic mindsets that shape our destinies. One is called "fixed mindset." People with this underlying concept of self believe that we are born with certain skills, traits, strengths, and weaknesses. Our characters, intelligence, and creative abilities are fixed, and if we're not good at or we fail at something, it's because we just don't have that talent.

The other is called "growth mindset." People with this underlying concept of self believe that we can change, learn, and grow as much as we want, as long as we're willing to put in the time and energy. We can develop our characters, grow our intelligence, and enhance our creative skills.

Guess which is true? Studies show that people with growth mindsets aren't forestalled by failure. They keep learning; they keep trying; they keep growing. They become more intelligent and more skilled. They really can achieve most anything they set out to. And best of all, they're happier. You can cultivate a growth mindset too. Pick something you want to learn and start working at it today.

*I have the capacity to change, learn,*
*and grow as much as I want to.*

# MARCH 22

*"Be patient toward all that is unsolved in your heart, and try to love the questions themselves, like locked rooms and like books that are written in a very foreign tongue. Do not now seek the answers, which cannot be given you because you would not be able to live them. And the point is to live everything. Live the questions now."*

— Rainer Maria Rilke

I have so many questions! Why do things have to be this way? Why now? Why this person and not that person? How does that work? What if this? What if that? What comes next?

It's only natural to ask such questions and search for answers. It's part of the human experience, wanting to know the whys and wherefores of life and beyond. That's why we have science, religion, and spirituality, which are attempts to come up with answers.

So let's keep seeking, but at the same time, let's also work on thriving in the unknowable. Many of our questions won't be answered in our lifetimes. This life, then, isn't for understanding everything, it's for "standing under" the mystery. It's for experiencing. This day is for living the questions.

*I have questions for which I may never receive answers, and so I will live the questions.*

# MARCH 23

*"Integrity is congruence between what you know,
what you profess, and what you do."*

— Nathaniel Branden

In the field of psychology, congruence is a term that describes acting in accordance with your beliefs and values. If you're congruent, you're walking your talk.

Most of us (with the exception of sociopaths) feel guilty or ashamed when we're not being congruent. If we believe it's important to recycle, for example, yet we throw our newspapers into the trash, we'll probably feel a tug of guilt every time we do it. If we profess to value kindness yet we're prone to name-calling or vindictive outbursts, we're bound to feel ashamed of ourselves afterward.

Congruence and mindfulness go hand-in-hand. If you're being incongruent, you're being unmindful because you're living a lie. Slow down today and be on the watch for tugs of incongruity. If you feel any, stop and correct your behavior. Notice how coming into congruity makes you feel.

*I choose to mindfully act in accordance
with my beliefs and values.*

# MARCH 24

*"You will do foolish things, but do them with enthusiasm."*
— Colette

Human life is a trial-and-error proposition. That's how we learn.
Oh sure, we can watch other people and heed their mistakes,
and we can read how-to articles and watch YouTube videos, but
at the end of the day, the best and only way to really, truly
learn something is to give it a whirl.

Thus all the dumb things we do. I've done my share. As a
parent, I try to impart my hard-won wisdom to my children,
but alas, they've got to make the same mistakes.
All I can do is cover my eyes and remember that I was
once as young and foolish as they are.

Besides, taking a risk is the only way to accomplish anything.
Often it doesn't work out, but that's OK. All we can do is apply
what we've learned and try again. And while we're at it, we might
as well go after the important stuff with enthusiasm. Tepid failure
is no fun. But passionate missteps? They're not missteps at all.
They're spirited lessons for the dance of our lives.

*I try and I learn. If I don't try, I don't learn.*
*I might as well try grandly so I can learn grandly.*

# MARCH 25

*"When you only have two pennies left in the world, buy a loaf of bread with one and a lily with the other."*

— Chinese Proverb

Pay attention to what you find beautiful. Things you are drawn to for their aesthetic value—such as art, music, nature, clothing, foods, experiences—are things your soul is calling out for.

Beauty lives in the now. Its very purpose, in fact, is to be experienced in the now. Stopping to appreciate it whenever you notice it is pleasurable mindfulness.

Try integrating more beauty into your life. Bring cut flowers or plants into your home. Buy or make art that inspires you. Listen to music while you shower or do dishes. Choose only clothing you love.

The lovelier your days, the more mindful your days. How can you make this day a little more lovely?

*I will mindfully add more beauty to my days.*

# MARCH 26

*"The thing about chameleoning your way through life is
that it gets to where nothing is real."*

— John Green

Are you a blender-inner? Do you feel more comfortable if you
can fade into the background, not attracting any attention to
yourself and not standing out in any way?

I believe you were put here to stand out. No, you don't have
to be a showboat. You don't have to ham it up or seek the
spotlight. But when it comes to your unique talents and
capacities, you do need to risk being seen.

What can you do that others find challenging. Do that, and
do it with aplomb! Step away from the background you're
chameleoning yourself against and say, "Here I am!"

The world needs you. *You* need you.
Be the real and fantastic individual you are.

*I have unique talents and capacities. I will mindfully
step forward so they can be seen and put to use.*

# MARCH 27

*"Organization isn't about perfection; it's about efficiency,
reducing stress and clutter, saving time and money,
and improving your overall quality of life."*

— Christina Scalise

A mindful life is an organized life.

It's virtually impossible to be mindful when you're surrounded
by chaotic clutter. What's more, clutter doesn't happen in the
first place if you're mindful. Before you set anything down, you
consider where it belongs, and you put it there.
If your awareness tells you the object is wholly
unnecessary, you give or throw it away.

Think of your home, your body (including grooming and
dress), and your administrative systems (for things like
paperwork—physical or electronic, bills, appointment calendar,
etc.) as physical manifestations of mindfulness.
How can you become more aware of each, treating it
with the intention and respect it deserves?

Organization, like mindfulness, is a habit that can
transform your life. Today, work on organizing one
tiny little thing. Tomorrow, another.

*I organize to mindfully improve my quality of life.*

# MARCH 28

*"As I walked out the door toward the gate that would lead
to my freedom, I knew if I didn't leave my bitterness
and hatred behind, I'd still be in prison."*

— Nelson Mandela

Bitterness can be understandable. Nelson Mandela was unjustly
imprisoned for 27 years—almost a third of his life! Of course he
was angry! Of course he harbored a grudge!

But by the time of his release, Mandela chose instead to live
from a place of peace and hope. He knew that bitterness
would only diminish his ability to live fully in the now of his
freedom. He understood that resentment would only continue
to imprison him. He was elected South Africa's first black
president, and he invited his former prison guards to the
inauguration. He also accepted the previous white president,
F.W. de Klerk, into his administration as first deputy.

When you feel resentment rise up inside you, remember Nelson
Mandela. Consider what you could mindfully accomplish in the
now if only you reconciled the bitternesses of the past.

*Bitterness and hatred only serve to imprison me.
I am working to reconcile them.*

# MARCH 29

*"Whatever the present moment contains, accept it as if you had chosen it. Always work with it, not against it."*

— Eckhart Tolle

Living in the now requires accepting what is.

If I get into a fender bender this afternoon (though I hope I don't!), I might be tempted to jump out of my car and emphatically confront the other driver to point out his mistake. But if instead I remember to remain mindful and accept what has happened, without unhelpful blaming or anxiety, I may be able to turn the situation into a net positive experience. I might notice that the other driver seems afraid or a little disoriented and needs compassionate care. I might reflect that I too have been a distracted driver at times, and there but for the grace of God go I.

We can strive this day to accept each moment as if we had chosen it. Barista got our coffee order wrong? That's OK. Let's consider the new version a lucky adventure. Unexpected news? That's OK. Let's resiliently look for the best path forward as well as silver linings.

*Today I will accept each moment as if I had chosen it.*

# MARCH 30

*"There is an eagle in me that wants to soar, and there is a
hippopotamus in me that wants to wallow in the mud."*

— Carl Sandburg

Today I want to talk about the virtues of the hippopotamus.
You see, it's essential to wallow when we need to wallow.
When the truth is that we're feeling sad or laid low by a
significant loss or challenge, mindfulness requires us to wallow
in that feeling. Sometimes our now is grief, and when that's
the case, we need to feel it to heal it.

So a little appropriate wallowing is essential. The danger comes
when we find ourselves getting stuck in the mud. If we're not
experiencing movement, we're not really living. Yes, we need
to pause and rest sometimes, but after a day, a week, a month,
or even a year of necessary stasis (depending on the
magnitude of the loss), it's time to get going again.

Intention and mindfulness can help us soar like an eagle again.
In between, we'll probably need to crawl like a turtle and amble
like an elephant, and we can make each of those phases
mindful as well. Which animal best represents your
inner truth today? Be that.

*Each day I mindfully encounter and honor
whatever I am feeling inside.*

# MARCH 31

*"Don't build a wall around your own suffering,*
*or it may devour you from the inside."*
— Frida Kahlo

Suffering is part of a mindful life. Actually, suffering is part of any human's life, because life invariably brings change, and change often results in loss. But when I say that suffering is part of a mindful life, what I really mean is that fully experiencing and expressing our natural suffering is mindful.

It's tempting to want to deny or avoid our pain. Here in America, we live in a grief-avoidant culture, so we encourage each other to bottle up "dark" emotions as we pursue our right to happiness. But what happens then? Our sadness, anger, guilt, and other challenging feelings don't go away. Oh no. What they do is devour us from the inside.

Emotional pain is as worthy of our awareness and exploration as joy. We're not living in the now until we're honestly living with *everything* in the now. Let's remember that today when something tough tugs on our heartstrings.

*I am knocking down the wall I have built around my*
*suffering so it stops devouring me from inside.*

# APRIL 1

*"It's a race between your foolishness and
your allotted days. Good luck."*

— Mark Slouka

Life flies by. The older we get, the faster it goes.

It's a race. But a race to what? I'd say it's a race to awakening.
Will we wake up before we die? Or will we remain among
the living dead until we draw our last breath?

The foolishness of mindlessly squandering our time is so
pervasive that it can seem like "the way things are" or even
"doing the right thing." And the true wisdom of mindfully
experiencing our time on earth is so uncommon that it,
conversely, can seem like foolishness.

Getting the two mixed up for too long is the most devastating
self-inflicted April Fool's prank of all time.

*I am racing to awaken and live awake.*

# APRIL 2

*"Why always 'not yet'? Do flowers in spring say 'not yet'?"*
— Norman Douglas

"Not yet" is nothing but a stall. So are "at some point," "maybe someday," and "when I get around to it."

Idle chatter and passing fancies are one thing.
It doesn't matter if you follow through on them or not.
But if you're talking about a true passion or dream,
procrastination is the height of hubris.

Today is all we're guaranteed. Mindfulness knows this.
Mindfulness takes action in the now. Only mindlessness stalls
and sputters along endlessly.

*Today is all I'm guaranteed. When it comes to things that matter
to me, I take action in the now.*

# APRIL 3

*"Hope and fear cannot occupy the same space at the same time. Invite one to stay."*

— Maya Angelou

Call to mind something you are fearful about. Allow yourself to wallow in your fear for a minute or two. Notice how it feels in your body.

Now call to mind something you feel hopeful about. Allow yourself to be buoyed by your hope for a minute or two. Notice how it feels in your body.

Which feels better? Which feels more mindful?

Fear is normal, and it is sometimes necessary (such as when we are in imminent danger), but too often we mindlessly give it more power than it deserves. We let it control too much of our lives. The next time we're feeling afraid, let's a) talk about it with someone who cares about us, then b) practice conjuring hope in its place. It's a smart switcheroo.

*I choose to mindfully cultivate hope instead of fear.*

# APRIL 4

*"Alice laughed. 'There's no use trying,' she said.*
*'One can't believe impossible things.'*

*'I daresay you haven't had much practice,' said the Queen.*
*'When I was younger, I always did it for half an hour a day.*
*Why, sometimes I've believed as many as six impossible*
*things before breakfast.'"*

— Lewis Carroll

What do you wish for that seems impossible?
Which wishes did you let go of in the past because you
deemed them impossible? How do you know they
are or were really impossible?

Often we unnecessarily limit ourselves (and others).
We tell ourselves it can't be done, so we don't even try.
We laugh at our own folly, and we carry on doing obviously
doable but underwhelming and unjoyful things instead.

Pick something you want (or used to want) that a) doesn't
require a lot of money and b) seems impossible.
Today, take one little step toward learning more about it. I bet
it's not impossible after all.

---

*Most everything I want is possible if I'm willing to mindfully*
*move it into the "possible" column.*

# APRIL 5

*"Impermanence is both a process of continual loss,*
*in which things exist and then disappear,*
*and it is also a process of continuous rebirth or creativity, in which*
*things that do not exist suddenly appear."*

— Joseph Goldstein

Resilience is the art of going with the flow. To a large extent, our lives are outside our control. Change is the only constant. Learning to mindfully acknowledge and adapt to change is essential to living in the now.

If you're not good at change, don't worry. You can change that!

Dr. Greg Eells, a psychologist at Cornell, coined the S.A.V.E.S method of developing resiliency: Social connection. Attitude. Values. Emotions. Silliness. Serving others and building social relationships, consciously choosing to cultivate a hopeful attitude, clarifying our deepest values, communicating about our emotions, and having the capacity to laugh at life and ourselves—all of these will help build our resilience. The next time you find yourself upset about change, remember SAVES. Practiced mindfully, it can save you.

*I choose to SAVES myself.*

# APRIL 6

*"After silence, that which comes nearest to*
*expressing the inexpressible is music."*
—Aldous Huxley

Ah, music. In my role as grief educator,
I often emphasize how important music is to helping us
access and feel our feelings. Somehow music opens us up. It
transcends language and speaks directly to our souls.

In our quest for mindfulness, music can help us
get out of our heads and into our hearts. It can help us
turn off our incessant thinking and be here now. That's why
background music is often used for meditation and prayer.

Try intentionally adding music to your day.
Choose music that helps you focus on whatever you need
most: inspiration, calm presence, memory work, etc.
If you need help finding the right music,
try Googling "music for _____."

*Mindfully choosing music and adding it to my day*
*helps me live in the now.*

# APRIL 7

*"Go and love someone exactly as they are and watch how
quickly they transform into the greatest, truest version of themselves.
When one feels seen and appreciated in their own essence, one is
instantly empowered."*

— Wes Angelozzi

Loving without judgment is a challenge for many of us.
We enter into relationships with certain expectations, and when
our partners, children, family members, or friends don't meet
those expectations, we feel disappointed or upset.

First, we should talk to our loved ones about our expectations.
Making them clear and visible is essential. For example:
"I expect you to call or text me if you'll be late
so that I don't worry."

And second, we should strive to let go of any expectations that
aren't necessary. Does it really matter if your son's hair is long
or your husband doesn't like to go to concerts with you? What
would happen if you loved them exactly as they are instead?
Besides, don't we want to be loved exactly as we are? Live and
let live. It's a mindful way to cherish the people we care about
and to help nurture their singular souls.

*I am mindfully working to love the people in my life
exactly as they are.*

# APRIL 8

*"You will not be punished for your anger.*
*You will be punished by your anger."*
— Buddha

Anger can be a tricky emotion. Like all human emotions, it is
normal and natural. We shouldn't be ashamed of our anger, but
neither should we let it control us. Rather, we should learn to
befriend it and learn from it.

Almost always, fear and hurt are the
foundational emotions that underlie anger. When we're
mad about something that happened at work or something
our child did, we're usually afraid that things won't
turn out as we hoped, or we're hurt that
we're being treated unfairly.

Mindfully exploring and expressing our anger requires us
to find constructive ways to help the heat dissipate. Lashing
out, for example, might feel like living in the now, but it is
not constructive. Going for a walk as we give attention to our
anger, on the other hand—that can be constructive. Once we're
calmer, we can mindfully discuss with others our feelings of
fear, hurt, and frustration.

*My anger is normal, but I must*
*mindfully explore and express it.*

# APRIL 9

*"Love is not an emotion. It's your very existence."*

— Rumi

Our feelings come and go, but real love persists.
It's not the same as our fleeting emotions, is it?
No, it's more like a meadow on top of which all our
emotions fly by like birds, with a flicker and a zip.

That's because we don't feel love, we *are* love. Love is our
essence. It's the fuel that burns our divine sparks.

When we're struggling with mercurial feelings, we can
acknowledge them while also seeking to find our steadfast love
within. It's in that place where we know that all is well and
that we are timelessly connected to others. Love is our very
existence. Love is our truest now.

*If I stop to center myself, I will find that love is*
*there as the foundation of every now.*

# APRIL 10

*"Paradise is thus not so much a place as liberation into the fullness and bounty of everyday experience."*

— Ian Baker

Once in a while I get a kick out of imagining heaven. I'll be talking with a friend, browsing online, reading a book, or watching a movie, and the subject will come up. "Oh yeah," I wonder. "What *could* it be like?"

Mindfulness helps us take that same thought process and apply it to the here and now. "Oh yeah," we remind ourselves when we remember to train our awareness on the current moment. "What *is* it like?"

When we live them with tender and grateful mindfulness, our everyday experiences often begin to feel like paradise. How lucky we are to be living right now, in this time and place, surrounded by these people! How spectacularly wonderful it all is!

What do we need to liberate ourselves from to live with this sense of wonder? Worry. Fear. Mindless attention to things that don't really matter and that we don't really care about.

*In this moment I can find paradise.*

# APRIL 11

*"You must take action now that will move you toward your goals.*
*Develop a sense of urgency in your life."*

— H. Jackson Brown, Jr.

Pick up a pen. In the space below, draw a horizontal line.
The left end of the line is when you were born. The right end of
the line is when you will die.

Now add a short vertical line, intersecting your horizontal line,
in the spot that you would guess indicates how much of your
life you have already lived. Circle the portion of the line that
represents the amount of time you have left.

Whatever your aspirations are, take action on them today.
Not tomorrow, today.

*Today I will take action that moves me toward my goals.*

# APRIL 12

*"We must accept finite disappointment but never lose infinite hope."*
— Dr. Martin Luther King, Jr.

Perhaps you've noticed that life doesn't
always go the way you'd planned.

No matter how mindfully and diligently we apply ourselves
to pursuing our goals, we can't always achieve what we set out
to achieve. And when it comes to random strokes of bad luck,
there's no telling what might happen and when.

Mindfully experiencing disappointment requires us to
acknowledge it, feel it, and find ways to integrate it into our
changed lives. Over time and with the support of others, we
reconcile ourselves to our new paths and rebuild hope.

How do you nurture hope? Devote some time to
hope-affirming activities today.

*I must reconcile myself to disappointment while
continuing to mindfully nurture hope.*

# APRIL 13

*"Over the years I have seen the power of taking an unconditional relationship to life, a willingness to show up for whatever life may offer, and meet with it rather than wishing to edit and change the inevitable… Perhaps the wisdom lies in engaging the life you have been given as fully and courageously as possible and not letting go until you find the unknown blessing that is in everything. I think that's how we have to practice."*

— Rachel Naomi Remen

Consciously, mindfully fostering an unconditional relationship with life is what this book is all about.

It's not always easy. Showing up for whatever happens and accepting what is can feel maddening at first. "What?" we think. "I'm just supposed to accept this? But I want to express my opinions! I want to change it!"

Expressing our feelings in the moment is good (as long as we're not being hurtful to others). But taking a deep breath, pausing, and asking ourselves what is really within our control to edit or change is also essential. Finally, we can remember to put things into the perspective of infinity.

Let's engage with life as fully and courageously as possible. Let's look for unknown blessings. Let's live mindfully this day.

*I am engaging with the life I have been given as fully and courageously as possible.*

# APRIL 14

*"Do you have patience to wait till your mud settles and the water is clear? Can you remain unmoving till the right action arises by itself?"*

— Lao Tzu

Stuff happens. Almost every day we're bombarded by a barrage of pesky troubles, and now and then a real doozy of a problem or loss knocks us ass-over-teakettle.

So what should we do about all of this heartache? How do we mindfully respond in the moment?

Patience is a response we can cultivate. If we wait to react, purposefully creating a gap between stimulus and response, maybe over the course of a day or a week or a month the mud will settle and the water will clear.

Maybe if we remain unmoving, breathing deeply and stilling ourselves, the right action will arise by itself.

*When I take the time to enter into mindfulness before reacting to a problem, pausing as long as necessary, the best solution often arises by itself.*

# APRIL 15

*"Your generosity toward others is key to your
positive experiences in the world.*

*Know that there's enough room for everyone to be passionate,
creative, and successful. In fact, there's more than room
for everyone; there's a need for everyone."*

— Marianne Williamson

If you're a precious child of God, and I'm a precious child of
God, then everyone on this earth is a precious child of God—
even those who have made bad choices or live mindlessly from
a place of hate or selfish ego.

Everyone belongs, and there's more than enough to go
around. We don't need to hoard riches for ourselves and
our loved ones. We should be generous, sharing freely
what we have so that no one will go without.

Generosity is mindful, and it feels good. Be generous to
someone you don't know well today, and notice how it makes
you feel about living in this world.

*I will be generous to others. There is enough for everyone to be
successful. We need everyone.*

# APRIL 16

*"The early bird gets the worm, but the second mouse gets the cheese."*
— Author Unknown

Progress has gifted us with free time. Only a few generations ago, most people had to spend every waking moment gathering food and ensuring their own survival. But now, almost everyone on the planet gets to enjoy at least some recreation and entertainment on a daily basis.

One problem now, of course, is that we have an overabundance of entertainment. There's so much to experience and enjoy that we can't possibly stay on top of it all. That's why we've developed FOMO—Fear Of Missing Out.

But here's the thing: we don't need to be an early bird. We don't need to get every worm. Too often, the first mouse loses itself to the pursuit, and the second mouse is the one that gets to relish the abundance.

Living in the now means arriving when we arrive, and experiencing what we experience. Striving to get there first or achieve trivial things is usually mindless.

*I don't need to be first. I don't need to know or experience everything. I will arrive when and where I arrive.*

# APRIL 17

*"The real goal of a spiritual tradition should not be ascent, but openness, vulnerability, and this does not require great experiences but, on the contrary, very ordinary ones. Charisma is easy; presence, self-remembering, is terribly difficult, and where the real work lies."*

— Morris Berman

In my own life, I know I'm sometimes guilty of focusing too much on Big Moments. When I speak to hundreds of people, for example, and am rewarded with a standing ovation, I'm delighted. It's not that I shouldn't feel proud and gratified at such times. It's just that I must work to remember that the highlights are not the main event. My day-to-day life, instead, is the main event.

Being present to our daily lives is where the real work lies. It's easier to be present while we're on vacation or attending a special event like a wedding, right? Yet our everyday existence is what really requires us to be here now.

Today let's work on being open and present in the most mundane of moments. Bonus points if we find sparks of the extraordinary in the ordinary.

*I am committed to being open and present in the most mundane of moments.*

# APRIL 18

*"You are never more fully yourself than when you are still."*
— Eckhart Tolle

Learning to still ourselves and return our focus to our divine sparks is an essential practice. It calms us and helps remind us of the often temporary or frivolous nature of whatever we may have been stressing out about beforehand.

When we retreat and grow still, we are working to connect with our essence. Inside each of us is what Tolle calls "unmanifested, unformed, unconditioned consciousness." In other words, who we were before we came into our bodies. Who we still are deep inside. Who we will always be.

Our truest selves are not anxious, busy, upset, judgmental, or hurtful. Instead, they are at ease, mindful, magnanimous, and loving. Let's carve out time to still ourselves today and be fully ourselves.

*Stillness helps me find and bring forth my true self.*

# APRIL 19

*"There are some unappreciated advantages to aging.*
*The very frailty of age guards its secrets. To many people you*
*become irrelevant, which gives you more time to do inner work."*

— Ram Dass

Vanity is mindless. When we spend too much time and
energy on our appearance, we're not experiencing the world,
connecting with others, or living out our passions. Instead,
we're mistaking our bodies for ourselves.

This isn't to say that our bodies aren't precious. They are
essential to our time here on earth, and so taking care of them
and enjoying them is also essential. But devoting ourselves to
our bodies is like spending day in and day out wrapping a gift
box when we have given absolutely no thought to the gift itself.

Usually the older we get, the more we realize that it's what
inside that counts. Our outsides may become irrelevant, but
inside we're doing the critical work of awakening.

*My insides are more important than my outsides.*
*I will apportion my time accordingly.*

# APRIL 20

*"Often in meditative language we speak of letting
go of things: let go of thoughts, let go of emotions, let go of pain.
Sometimes that is not exactly the right phrase,
because letting go suggests that you need to do something.
A better phrase to work with is 'Let it be.' Everything comes and
goes by itself. We do not have to do anything to make it come,
or make it go, or to let it go. We just have to let it be."*

— Joseph Goldstein

Living in the now means acknowledging, accepting, and
experiencing what is. Joseph Goldstein is right—it's not about
"letting go" of thoughts and emotions; it's about encountering
them and allowing them to be.

Everything belongs, even the "bad" stuff.

Anger? Allow it to be, and befriend it.
Jealousy? Allow it to be, and befriend it.
Sadness? Allow it to be, and befriend it.

Today, whatever comes up for you, allow it to be
without feeling you have to do anything with it
besides embrace it.

*I spend my days not letting things go
but instead experiencing them.*

# APRIL 21

*"Do not think that what your thoughts dwell upon is of no matter.*
*Your thoughts are making you."*

— Bishop Steere

In our mindfulness journey, we become more and
more aware that our stream-of-consciousness
thoughts are ruling our lives.

"I'm late," we think. "I'm fat. Ooh, that house is nice.
Too expensive, though. And I haven't saved enough for
retirement. That person is better (or worse) than me.
I wonder what's on Netflix?"

Giving our monkey minds free rein is the very
definition of mindlessness. Only when we learn to pay no heed
to our errant thoughts and instead train our minds to help us
carry out our deepest desires and live fully, with gratitude,
in the now are we are practicing mindfulness.

Our thoughts are making us. What do you think?

*When I am mindless, my thoughts are making me.*
*When I am mindful, I rise above my thoughts and live with*
*intention and gratitude in the now.*

# APRIL 22

*"I do believe in an everyday sort of magic—the inexplicable connect-edness we sometimes experience with places, people, works of art and the like; the eerie appropriateness of moments of synchronicity; the whispered voice, the hidden presence, when we think we're alone."*

— Charles de Lint

The more present we become,
the more aware we become of the synchronicities
that arise all around us. We suddenly see the same number over
and over again or hear a certain piece of music
everywhere we go. We think of a particular friend
and then that friend calls us. We need something and
soon it appears, seemingly out of the blue.

I believe such synchronicities aren't mere coincidence.
Rather, I think they're gifts meant to reassure us that everything
makes sense. We may never fully comprehend the mystery
while we're here on earth, but we can live with awareness that
we are "standing under" the mystery.

Watch for everyday magic, and regard it with wonder.

*My heightened awareness is helping me experience more and
more everyday magic.*

# APRIL 23

*"I don't want to get to the end of my life and find that I lived just the length of it. I want to have lived the width of it as well."*

— Diane Ackerman

31,000. If you live to 85, that's how many days you will have been privileged to spend on this earth.

Have you ever noticed that we ascribe a lot of meaning to the length of a person's life? We generally consider 85 years a good lifespan. Anything over 90 is fantastic, right? Anything under about 60 is way too short, and anything under about 30 is a tragedy.

But isn't the width of a life just as (if not more) important than the length? Isn't what we do with our days sometimes a more effective measure than the quantity of days?

You've got 24 hours until you turn to the next page in this book. Live the width of them.

*I promise to live the width of my days.*

# APRIL 24

*"Do not ruin today with mourning tomorrow."*
— Catherynne M. Valente

Mourning is a normal, necessary thing.
When we're grieving inside, we need to express our grief
outside of ourselves in order to heal. This is called mourning.
Mourning has the power to help us transcend our grief and go
on to live and love fully again.

But sometimes we grieve and mourn without good reason.
Usually this is because we're apprehensive about something that
*might* happen at some point in the future. We worry, which puts
us in the future instead of the now. And some of us seem to live
in a constant state of anxiety.

If your todays are consumed by worries about tomorrow,
you won't be able to live mindfully. So it's probably time to see
a counselor. A few therapy sessions may be enough to provide
you with tools to better manage your anxiety.
Your today is waiting for you.

*I can only live today if I stop worrying about tomorrow.*

# APRIL 25

*"A ship is safe in the harbor, but that's not what ships are for."*
— Author Unknown

A person who takes no risks and loves no one is safe,
but that's not what people are for.

What are *you* for? Why are you here? What do you bring to
those around you? What makes you vibrate with aliveness?
What is your calling? You're here for reasons, of that I am sure.

Discovering and staying mindful of your purposes is
your daily task. Taking risks and launching yourself into
unknown waters in pursuit of your purposes is
also mindfulness in action.

Untie yourself from the comfort of your dock and set sail.

*Mooring myself safe in the harbor is not what my life is for.*

# APRIL 26

*"I had thought joy to be rather synonymous with happiness, but it seems now to be far less vulnerable than happiness. Joy seems to be a part of an unconditional wish to live, not holding back because life may not meet our preferences and expectations. Joy seems to be a function of the willingness to accept the whole, and to show up to meet with whatever is there. It has a kind of invincibility that attachment to any particular outcome would deny us."*

— Rachel Naomi Remen

My editor tells me that her grandmother, whom she called Nana, was the most joyful person she ever knew. By her early 60s, Nana's husband had died. She lived alone in a modest house in a small town in Minnesota. Her life seemed like nothing special, but she veritably fizzed with delight and engagement.

Nana loved to garden, play Scrabble, and drink tea. She walked at least two miles a day well into her 80s. She greeted everyone she knew with an infectious smile and an exclamation about what a glorious day it was, regardless of the weather.

Nana's unfailingly joyous mindfulness helped her weather setbacks and losses. Bad things happened along the way. She wasn't always happy, certainly, but she was always happy to see *you*, and she remained hopeful and grateful. I wish I'd met her.

*I may not always be happy, but I can always be joyful.*

# APRIL 27

*"I slept and dreamt that life was joy.*
*I awoke and saw that life was service.*
*I acted and behold, service was joy."*
— Rabindranath Tagore

The more present we become, the more we understand that
service to others is the most meaningful way of all to
spend our present moments.

That's because our connections to others are what gives life the
most meaning. Don't believe me? Take this test: You learn you
have one more day to live. You can either spend your day alone
in an exotic, sumptuous location of your choice, or you can stay
at home with the people you love most.

Love and kindness power our souls. Serving others is the most
loving act. Therefore, serving others powers our souls like
nothing else can. Of course, we must balance service to others
with good self-care. Retreating to mindfully
recharge ourselves is also necessary.

Life is service is joy.
Test the theory by serving someone today.

*Helping others brings me joy.*
*Love and kindness power my soul.*

# APRIL 28

*"In my walks, I would fain return to my senses.*
*What business have I in the woods if I am thinking*
*of something out of the woods?"*

— Henry David Thoreau

Spending time in nature helps restore us to ourselves.

I dare you to go for a walk in the woods or another natural area
today without your cell phone. Allow at least an hour.
Walk and walk and walk.

As you walk, observe your surroundings. Absorb the place
and the experience with all five of your senses. Shoo away any
thoughts that might arise about your to-do list. Happily return
to your senses. Invite deeper matters of
the soul to come to the surface.

It's harder to be mindless in the woods.
Thoreau knew that. You can know it too.

*When I spend time in nature, I am more present and mindful.*

# APRIL 29

*"Feeling compassion for ourselves in no way
releases us from responsibility for our actions.
Rather, it releases us from the self-hatred that prevents us from
responding to our life with clarity and balance."*

— Tara Brach

God knows we're not perfect. In working to live mindfully,
we're on the path. We're journeyers, but we're not masters.
And even masters make mistakes.

When we mess up (and we will), the mindful response is
twofold: 1) Take responsibility. Say sorry and make amends.
And 2) Practice self-compassion. Acknowledge that human
beings make mistakes. Express our regrets, explore what we can
do differently next time, and forgive ourselves. Yes, we can be
both self-responsible and self-compassionate.

Carrying self-hatred forward will only prevent us from living
mindfully in the days to come. The people we care about—
heck, the whole world—needs us fully
present and accounted for.

*I take responsibility for my actions, and I forgive myself.*

# APRIL 30

*"Dealing With Anything:*
*1. Mope*
*2. Cope*
*3. Hope"*

—Amy Krouse Rosenthal

At the age of 50, bestselling children's author Amy Krouse
Rosenthal was diagnosed with Stage 4 ovarian cancer.
She died a year later.

In just a few short words, Rosenthal reminds us that whenever
something challenging happens in our lives, we will find our
way through if we follow this sequence: First we mope. We take
time to withdraw, acknowledge our new reality, and embrace
our hard feelings. Then we cope. We learn to live our daily lives
even as we continue to grieve and mourn, with the support
of others. And finally we hope. We may still be moping and
coping, but we're also expecting good things in our futures.
We're both living our now and setting our intention for the joys
and happy surprises ahead of us.

When I was diagnosed with prostate cancer in 2011, I moped, I
coped, and I hoped. I now live a life of joy and happiness.

Mope. Cope. Hope. It may be the only mantra we need.

*Whenever I encounter a challenge,*
*I will remember to mope, cope, and hope.*

# MAY 1

*"The flower doesn't dream of the bee. It blossoms and the bee comes."*
— Mark Nepo

What do you dream of for your life? What are your most
audacious hopes and desires?

You're here. Your dreams are over there.
How do you bridge the gap?

You blossom. You set your intention to fulfill your destiny,
then you begin to open yourself. You take small, one-day-at-a-
time actions that help you unfurl. You learn a bit. You try a bit.
You go out on a limb a bit. You reach out to others a bit.
You enjoy the process. Repeat daily.

If you mindfully blossom,
your bees will begin to come to you.

*Day by day, I am mindfully blossoming.*

# MAY 2

*"Do every act of your life as though
it were the last act of your life."*
— Marcus Aurelius

Mindfulness demands full and focused attention on
whatever we're doing at the moment.

When we're being mindless, we're allowing our minds to
separate from our bodies. Our bodies are here doing one thing,
and our minds are off thinking about something else.
Or we're allowing our minds to catastrophize about what our
bodies are experiencing. (I'm riding my bike. Oh no, the last
time I rode my bike I fell. I'm probably going to fall again, but
this time I'll get badly hurt…)

Our mindfulness practice asks us to keep our minds and bodies
together and to become aware of thought patterns that take us
too far afield from our in-the-moment reality. For most of us, it's
exhausting at first, living in the now. But like a muscle,
the more we use it, the stronger it gets.

*I am present to every act of my life.*

# MAY 3

*"One does not become enlightened by imagining figures of light but by making the darkness conscious. The latter procedure, however, is disagreeable and therefore not popular."*

— Carl Jung

I've been a grief counselor and death educator for about forty years, so I know how unpopular loss and death generally are in our culture. We don't like to think or talk about them. They're the proverbial elephant in the room.

But loss and death are normal and necessary. They're as much a part of life as love and birth. And it's only when we live from a place of awareness of both extremes—life and death— that we begin to live fully.

What darknesses do you have within you that you need to make conscious? If you have any suppressed emotions or experiences inside you that feel like grief, sadness, hate, anger, guilt, envy, and/or shame, bringing them mindfully to the fore through intentional awareness, exploration, and expression is a necessary step on the journey to enlightenment.

Making the darkness conscious may feel disagreeable at first, but once you feel the momentum it unleashes, you'll come to be grateful for its healing power.

*I am working to make my darkness conscious.*

# MAY 4

*"The truth is like a lion. You don't have to defend it.
Let it loose. It will defend itself."*

— St. Augustine

The truth has a way of making itself known.

When we're mindfully present, especially,
the truth nudges us. "I'm here," it says.
"I'm ready for you to give me your full awareness."

Whatever our most essential truths are, we don't need to defend
or justify them. We just have to be ourselves. Because when we
are mindfully ourselves, in the now, we are living on purpose.
We are living in congruence with our beliefs, values,
passion, and personality.

Your truth is like a lion. Let it roar.

*I don't have to defend or justify my truth.
I only have to let it loose.*

# MAY 5

*"There is no waste in the world that equals the waste from
needless, ill-directed, and ineffective motions."*

— Frank Bunker Gilbreth, Sr.

In today's quotation, Frank Gilbreth is encouraging us to be
strategically effective in everything we do. But here's the thing…
How are we ever going to learn what's effective and what's not if
we don't try various approaches and
make mistakes along the way?

Effectiveness matters to me, because I believe each of us has at
least one purpose to fulfill. But sometimes figuring out what
that purpose is, and how best to fulfill it, is a messy process.

On the other hand, we've all known people who seem to
misspend their entire lives on needless, ill-directed pursuits that
do not give them a sense of meaning and purpose.

So don't be afraid to try and to fail, but if you feel like you're
spinning your wheels for too long, also don't be afraid to seek
out support and life coaching. Sometimes getting unstuck
is the most effective move to make next.

*When I'm spinning my wheels for too long,
I will seek out support and help.*

# MAY 6

*"As often happens on the spiritual journey, we have arrived at the heart of a paradox: Each time a door closes, the rest of the world opens up. All we need to do is stop pounding on the door that has just closed, turn around—which puts the door behind us—and welcome the largeness of life that now lies open to our souls. The door that closed kept us from entering a room, but what now lies before us is the rest of reality."*

— Parker Palmer

Whenever doors close in our lives, it's natural and normal for us to grieve. It takes time and mindful attention to our grief for us to incorporate the loss into our identities and become ready to move forward as changed people.

The trick is to be vulnerable enough to change and our lack of control that when doors close, we surrender with as much grace as possible. We acknowledge and express our grief, and we work with intention to open our arms to all the good that is yet to be.

Our lives can be large and contain many rooms, if only we'll keep opening more doors.

*My life is large and contains many rooms.
I will keep opening new doors.*

# MAY 7

*"If you don't like where you are, move. You're not a tree."*

— Jim Rohn

Stillness is part of our mindfulness practice. Each day we find ways to calm and center ourselves so that we can reconnect with the deepest, truest parts of ourselves.

But then we move! We take action! We actively love and care for others. We share our gifts with the world.
We pursue our goals and fulfill our purpose.
We ask for help when we need help.

Whenever we're feeling stuck, let's remember our mindfulness two-step: 1). Center. 2). Move.

We're not trees. If we want to, we can change ourselves, we can change our circumstances, and we can change the world.
What a glorious opportunity.

*If I don't like where I am,*
*I can move.*

# MAY 8

*"Progressive improvement beats delayed perfection."*
— Mark Twain

Raise your hand if you have a tendency to not try things because
you know you're not any good at them.
My hand is in the air. Is yours?

Let's remember that in the now, we're still learning. We can only
ever accomplish progressive improvement in the now.
Nobody goes from beginner to master in a moment.

And without progressive improvement, mastery is unattainable.
Delayed perfection is a myth. There is no such thing as
perfection, but even near-perfect can't be achieved without lots
of practice and mistakes along the way.

Living in the now means taking imperfect action in the now,
one day at a time. The gratifying thing is that imperfect actions,
over time, accumulate into near-perfect mastery.
So please, make a smidge of improvement today.

*I am improving infinitesimal bit
by infinitesimal bit, day by day.*

# MAY 9

*"You might be tempted to avoid the messiness of daily living
for the tranquility of stillness and peacefulness.
This of course would be an attachment to stillness, and like any
strong attachment, it leads to delusion. It arrests development and
short-circuits the cultivation of wisdom."*

— Jon Kabat-Zinn

The word "mindfulness" sometimes conjures the wise guru on
the mountaintop. He sits in peace and isolation, meditating his
days away and occasionally dispensing sage advice to seekers
who risk life and limb to find him.

This brand of misanthropic mindfulness is alluring to some
people. They love the idea of retreating from society as much as
possible and spending most of their time alone,
in quiet contemplation.

I understand. I regularly make time to recharge in solitude.
But I also know that I need the messiness of daily living: to
love other people, to serve, to challenge myself, to grow, and to
cultivate true wisdom. Mindfulness is not about retreating from
human society but rather engaging with it intentionally.

*I need both tranquility and participation in life. I go back and
forth as I mindfully work to live fully.*

# MAY 10

*"When you are here and now, not jumping ahead, the miracle has
happened. To be in the moment is the miracle."*

— Osho

Honing our ability to live in the moment helps us not only be
present to our lives, it also helps us separate meaningless stress
from what really matters. And figuring out what really
matters each day will help us live fully the
remainder of our precious days.

One way to work on living in the moment is an exercise called
"notice five things." When you're feeling stressed or distracted,
stop whatever it is you're doing. Still yourself. Take five deep,
slow, in-and-out breaths. Now look around you. Silently name
five things you can see. Next name five things you can hear.
Then name five things you can feel, inside or outside your body.
Then name five things you can smell. Even if you're not actively
eating or drinking, if you try you can probably name several
lingering tastes in your mouth.

After you're done noticing five things, take a temperature on
your thoughts and emotions. Has your anxiety dissipated a
little? Are you feeling a bit more centered and calm?
I know I am.

*Noticing five things helps return me to the now.*

# MAY 11

*"You can have compassion for yourself—which is not self-pity.
You're simply recognizing that 'this is tough, this hurts,' and bringing
the same warmhearted wish for suffering to lessen or end that you
would bring to any dear friend grappling with the same pain,
upset, or challenges as you."*

— Rick Hanson

Today or whenever necessary, I give you permission
to feel deeply sorry for yourself.

Life often hurts. Bad things happen. Change is the only
constant, and we frequently lose things and
people that matter to us.

When others around us experience loss, we feel bad for them.
We empathize. We put ourselves in their shoes and try to
understand their experience from their point of view.
We treat them with compassion.

When we ourselves experience loss, we must practice self-
empathy and self-compassion. We must mindfully acknowledge
our own struggles and affirm our need to grieve and mourn in
the now. If we don't, we simply cannot live and love fully again.

*I treat myself with the same empathy and compassion
I would extend to a dear friend.*

# MAY 12

*"Sometimes the bad things that happen in our lives put us
directly on the path to the best things
that will ever happen to us."*

— Nicole Reed

Since I'm a death and grief guy, hundreds of people have shared
some variation on this message with me over the years:
From our greatest wounds come our greatest gifts.

I'm always quick to affirm that such gifts are bittersweet. If
someone we love dies and we become a better person as a
result, for example, that doesn't mean our personal growth
made everything worth it. We'd often happily exchange all the
benefits for just one more minute with the person who died.

For example, a well-intentioned person once said to me, "It's a
good thing your friend died when you were a teen. You have
written some really helpful books." My thought:
"Forget the books. I'll take my friend back."

Still, when something bad happens, we can intentionally
envision the good that might come from it. We can foster our
inner knowing that all is well. We can mindfully work to put
ourselves on the path that leads where we want to go.

*Bad can lead to good. This is part of my intention.*

# MAY 13

*"Self-respect is the root of discipline: the sense of dignity that grows with the ability to say no to oneself."*

— Abraham Joshua Heschel

In the now, we have a myriad of choices to make. What to wear, what to eat, whom to talk to, what to read, where to go, what to do, what not to do. Sometimes we mistakenly believe that living in the now means choosing to say yes to every opportunity for pleasure that might present itself. Sure, I'll watch another episode. Yes, I'll sleep in. Of course I want a beer!

But true mindfulness requires discipline. If you are aware, you are weighing your moment-to-moment choices on one side of the scale that holds your goals and responsibilities on the other. Saying yes to too many opportunities for pleasure in the moment might mean saying no to paying your rent or pursuing your calling.

As each choice in your day presents itself, work to mindfully balance short-term gratification and long-term satisfaction. You can and should have both. I've noticed, though, that for many people, the seesaw often tips mindlessly to the former, leading to unfortunate long-term challenges and unhappiness.

*I respect and love myself, so I give myself the gift of self-discipline.*

# MAY 14

*"It is never late to ask yourself,*
*'Am I ready to change my life, am I ready to change myself?'*
*However old we are, whatever we went through, it is always possible*
*to be reborn. If each day is a copy of the last one, what a pity!*
*Every breath is a chance to be reborn. But to be reborn into a new*
*life, you have to die before dying."*

— Shams Tabrizi

When is the best time to launch a
self-improvement project? Now.

That's a trick question, of course, because we're conditioned to
say "Monday" or "after our vacation" or "January 1." We've been
culturally trained to believe that we have to allow time to psych
ourselves up and get our procrastinating out of our systems.
But that's not true. We can start really small,
and we can start right now. Every day is a new chance, true.
But what's more true is that every breath is a new chance.
All we have to do is act.

*Every breath I take is a new chance to begin.*

# MAY 15

*"He who is of a calm and happy nature will hardly feel the pressure of age, but to him who is of an opposite direction, youth and age are equally a burden."*

— Plato

The mindfulness habit we're nurturing together enhances the quality of our lives, but did you know it can also influence the *quantity* of our lives?

A recent study by Nobel-winning scientist Elizabeth Blackburn confirms that our bodies age more quickly when our thought patterns tend to be hostile, pessimistic, or ruminative (thinking about the same problems over and over). Interestingly, cellular aging also speeds up when we habitually suppress difficult thoughts and feelings and when we too often allow our minds to wander, thinking about things other than what we're currently engaged in, especially if those things are negative.

Awareness helps us identify these harmful thought patterns and return us to the now. In the now we can work to be calm, optimistic, acknowledging of our true emotions, and present. It feels better, and we just might live longer.

*Mindfulness helps me feel better and maybe even live longer.*

# MAY 16

*"You have been criticizing yourself for years, and it hasn't worked.
Try approving of yourself and see what happens."*

— Louise Hay

A central tenet of living in the now is acceptance of what is.
This means, of course, that acceptance of ourselves as
we are in the now is also essential.

Right now, take an inventory of everything you currently don't
like about yourself. Coming up with a nice long list? Me too.

Let's run through our lists again, but this time,
let's put the words "I approve of" in front of each item.
I approve of my paunch. I approve of my volatility.
I approve of my failures to meditate.

There. Now that we're approving of ourselves in the now, we
can actually inhabit the now. We can still mindfully work to
make the best choices each day,
but no matter what, we're OK as is.

*I approve of myself as I am.*

# MAY 17

*"The most exhausting thing in life is being insincere."*
— Anne Morrow Lindbergh

One thing our mindfulness practice should foster is a sense
of ease and comfort. The more aware we are of our thoughts,
feelings, and surroundings, the more readily we can make
choices that align with our divine sparks.
The more at home we feel in our own skins.

Have you ever worn clothing that was stylish but didn't feel like
"you"? It's uncomfortable, right? That's what insincerity feels
like. It chafes, and it acts as a barrier between our truth and
how we interact with the world. It prevents us from being fully
present to our own unique lives.

Let's work to be genuine. No lies. No masks. No false pretenses.
Just our true selves being open, honest, and vulnerable.

*Only when I am being sincere am I fully present.*

# MAY 18

*"Yesterday.*

*Now.*

*Tomorrow."*

— Author Unknown

This quotation would make a great tattoo,
if you're the tattooing sort, which I am not.

What I think is interesting about it is that it could
just say "Now." That simple, one-word mantra might be enough
to help us return to the moment over and over again.
Now. Now. Now.

But when we picture the Now sandwiched between Yesterday
and Tomorrow, we're given guardrails. Actually, I imagine
them more like the rumble strips you find on the edges of
some highways. If we're working to envision this quotation
and our minds veer off the path of Now and onto Yesterday or
Tomorrow, we immediately feel that rumble warning us that
we're headed into dangerous territory.

Not Yesterday. Not Tomorrow. Now.

*Not yesterday. Not tomorrow. Now.*

# MAY 19

*"Feeling gratitude and not expressing it is
like wrapping a present and not giving it."*
— William Arthur Ward

Gratitude has two parts. One part is what we think and
feel inside when we are grateful for someone or something.
Sometimes we feel it spontaneously, in the moment, and
sometimes we foster its emergence through intentional
activities, such as gratitude journaling.

The other part of gratitude is its expression back to the person
who is responsible for whatever it is we feel grateful about. It's
the closing of the loop, if you will.

Both parts help us with our mindfulness practice.
Both parts help us live in and appreciate the now. But the
second part provides the additional benefit of strengthening
our connections with others and helping them become
more mindful in their own lives.

Gratitude expressed is indeed a gift. It's a gift for us, and it's a
gift for the good-deed-doer. I try to express heartfelt
gratitude at least once each day. I hope you'll join me.

*I will express heartfelt gratitude one or more times every day.*

# MAY 20

*"It's the very pursuit of happiness that thwarts happiness."*
— Viktor Frankl

Viktor Frankl was a prominent Jewish psychiatrist who lived in Vienna. In 1942 he and his family were sent to a Nazi concentration camp. He survived. His family, including his pregnant wife, did not.

Frankl later wrote a famous book entitled *Man's Search for Meaning* about his Holocaust experience. In it he explained that the people who were most likely to survive the camps were those who held onto a sense of purpose. Their happiness, in turn, flowed from pursuing and realizing that purpose.

When we mindfully acknowledge, nurture, and pursue our deepest purposes, we find happiness. When we try to take a shortcut straight to happiness, on the other hand, we're left feeling empty and a nagging sense of unfulfillment. The pursuit of happiness actually leads to unhappiness.

Happiness research bears this out.

And so in the now, we're directing our awareness to make choices that lead to meaning instead of instant happiness.

*I seek meaning, not happiness.*

# MAY 21

*"Mantra is that which projects the mind in a fixed direction."*
— Yogi Bhajan

Have you tried committing a short phrase of intention to memory and repeating it to yourself over and over again, aloud or in your mind, either during meditation or as you go about your daily business?

Such a phrase is called a "mantra," and research shows that repeated use of mantras creates physical pathways in our brains. The more repetitions, the stronger the circuit grows. It's like walking the same path in your lawn over and over again. The more it's walked, the more well-worn it becomes.

In studies, repeated use of positive mantras has been shown to lower stress hormones, increase endurance, and produce a feeling of calmness. Try out several mantras with different emphases. Keep them short and positive. Mindfully work on the habit of putting your mantras to work at stressful times.

A word of caution: If using positive mantras creates powerful pathways, that means negative self-talk creates equally powerful pathways.

*I use positive mantras throughout my day.*

# MAY 22

*"Begin doing what you want to do now. We are not living in eternity. We have only this moment, sparkling like a star in our hand —and melting like a snowflake."*

— Francis Bacon

When is it the right time to do what you want to do? If it's something you deeply yearn for, the right time is always now— or as soon thereafter as humanly possible.

We're not guaranteed next year, next week, or tomorrow. Heck, we're not even guaranteed the remainder of today.

Francis Bacon's image of the melting snowflake can help us remember our mortality. When we're feeling stuck or frustrated or mindless, we can turn a palm face up. In this palm, we can imagine a single snowflake. The snowflake is this one precious moment, and it is already beginning to melt.

So what are we going to do to make the most of it?

*I have only this moment, sparkling like a star in my hand and melting like a snowflake.*

# MAY 23

*"Don't meditate to fix yourself, to heal yourself, to improve yourself,
to redeem yourself; rather, do it as an act of love, of deep, warm
friendship to yourself. In this way there is no longer any need for
the subtle aggression of self-improvement, for the endless guilt of not
doing enough. It offers the possibility of an end to the ceaseless round
of trying so hard that wraps so many people's lives in a knot. Instead
there is now meditation as an act of love. How endlessly
delightful and encouraging."*

— Bob Sharples

We might meditate for many reasons, but the simplest and
perhaps most pure reason is simply to love ourselves.

Meditation and meditative activities such as yoga are forms of
self-care. We care for ourselves because we love ourselves and
deserve excellent self-care.

So try meditating without agenda. Meditate joyfully, without
attachment to outcome. Simply do it knowing that
it's loving self-care.

*When I meditate, I am loving myself.*

# MAY 24

*"Be careful how you are talking to yourself because*
*you are listening."*

— Lisa M. Hayes

All of us talk to ourselves. Some of us even do it out loud.

Sometimes we're overly harsh with ourselves, and sometimes
we're overly generous. We tell ourselves we're dumb, lazy,
unattractive, bad. Or we tell ourselves we're right,
more successful, smarter.

Negative self-talk is harmful because it shames us into settling
for our worst selves. Overly generous self-talk is harmful
because it's often our egos reassuring us that
we're better than others.

The truth is that each of us is gloriously imperfect. We can and
should take risks to be our best possible selves each day. And
we should also remember that we're no better than anyone else.
Our self-talk is most mindful when it embraces this paradox.

*I am mindful of how I talk to myself—because I am listening.*

# MAY 25

*"We are not troubled by things but by the opinions*
*we have about things."*

— Epictetus

Life can be a pain in the you-know-what, but it's often our
thoughts that create the real problems.

When something annoying or unexpected happens, do you ever
blow it out of proportion? I know I do. Often our thoughts and
opinions about what happened cause the real kerfuffle—
not the happening itself.

The next time we feel ourselves getting annoyed or anxious
about something, let's try to separate that something from
our thoughts about it. Mindfulness can help us tease the two
things apart. Practicing heightening our awareness of our own
responses can help us tame them.

*When I strip away the thoughts I have about something, I can*
*encounter the truth of it instead.*

# MAY 26

*"When we are in the midst of chaos, let go of the need to control it.
Be awash in it, experience it in that moment, try not to control the
outcome but deal with the flow as it comes."*

— Leo Babauta

This is a biggie: Mindfulness is not the same thing as control.

In the moment, being mindful does *not* mean using the
capacities of our minds to control others or situations. Instead,
being mindful means being present to and aware of whatever is
happening and choosing our responses with intentionality. In
other words, we do not seek to control our days.
We seek to be fully present in them.

We can learn to live in the now with chaos, encountering it
with full awareness, being awash in it. We can sometimes
create a pause before responding with equal mindfulness.
This pause is a form of control within ourselves, but it is
not an attempt to control the situation. This is an essential
distinction for us to remember.

*I am mindful of the now, but I cannot control the now.*

# MAY 27

*"If you hear a voice within you say you cannot paint, then by all means paint and that voice will be silenced."*

— Vincent Van Gogh

Self-doubt hampers most of us at one time or another. Often because of beliefs we internalized, consciously or unconsciously, in our childhoods, we think we are incapable of certain things. We believe we lack abilities or talents, even though we may yearn to do those very things.

Studies show that most of the things we think of as talents or inborn personality traits are in fact learned skills. It turns out that the concept of fixed mindset is based on falsehoods. With a growth mindset, on the other hand, you understand the truth: that everyone is capable of learning, changing, and growing.

If you want to paint, you can learn to paint. If you want to _____, you can learn to _____. Mindfully cultivate your growth mindset today and every day.

*If I hear a voice within me saying I cannot_____,*
*then by all means I should _____*
*and that voice will be silenced.*

# MAY 28

*"What you resist, persists."*

— Carl Jung

Feelings of resistance within us are clues that something needs our attention. They're kind of like psychological snags. Whenever we feel that tug of something sticking, our goal should be to mindfully turn our awareness to it and try to figure out how to unsnag it.

Let's say we're angry at someone but we've been avoiding having a difficult conversation with this person about our anger. Resisting our anger doesn't make it go away, does it? In fact, it sometimes compounds it. But if we muster the courage to mindfully express our anger in the now, it may begin to dissipate.

Learning to acknowledge and address our own feelings of resistance in the moment, as they arise, is an essential part of our mindfulness practice. We are not living fully in the now if we are avoiding aspects of the now. The now is comprised of the full gamut of experiences and feelings—good, bad, and indifferent. We must be equally present to all of it.

*When I feel myself resisting or avoiding, I know I have found something that needs my presence and expression.*

# MAY 29

*"The most precious gift we can offer others is our presence.*
*When mindfulness embraces those we love,*
*they will bloom like flowers."*

— Thich Nhat Hanh

Mindfulness isn't just about how we experience life. It's also about how others experience life when they are in our presence.

Our energy impacts those around us. When we are mindful, our openness, genuineness, and kindness are felt by other people. We acknowledge them. We look them in the eye. We smile. The divine in us honors the divine in them. Consciously or unconsciously, they pick up on our way of being and are more likely to enter into an equable state of presence alongside us.

When we choose to turn our full awareness onto others, inviting them to converse with us and giving them our complete attention, we are like the sun shining on them. Our hospitality opens them up, and in our presence we may have the privilege of seeing them bloom like flowers.

*The most precious gift I can offer others is my presence.*

# MAY 30

*"Rather than being your thoughts and emotions,*
*be the awareness behind them."*

— Eckhart Tolle

Our divine sparks are our timeless, imperturbable essence.
Deep down inside, we know that we are privileged
to come from a loving source—a source to which we will
return when our earthly days have elapsed.
No matter what happens, all is well.

But we naturally experience lots of thoughts and feelings
along the way, too. It's part of being human. In large part our
mindfulness practice is about learning to take one step back
from our all-over-the-place thoughts and feelings and observe
them with empathy and non-judgment.

At our core is pure, unflappable awareness.
We will work to live from that core today.

*I am not my thoughts and emotions.*
*I am the awareness behind them.*

# MAY 31

*"There's never enough time to do all the nothing you want."*
— Bill Watterson

As you make your way through this year of mindfulness with me, you'll soon realize that I'm a *carpe diem* kind of guy. Life is for seizing. Our precious days here are numbered, and it's a shame if we don't make the most of each and every one of them.

And yet, well-wasted time is also an essential part of the mix. Trying to make every moment productive is counterproductive. First of all, when we're too regimented, we miss out on happenstance and spontaneity. We're also likely to be constantly thinking about the next task on our to-do list instead of fully immersing ourselves in the present activity.

What's more, research shows that naps and other mental breaks (Netflix, anyone?) enhance our productivity, solidify our memories, replenish our attention, and nurture our creativity. The best strategy seems to be to build in little breaks throughout the day and deliberately set aside technology at regular intervals.

*I need breaks and downtime in between times of mindful productivity.*

# JUNE 1

*"Make the most of yourself by fanning the tiny, inner sparks
of possibility into flames of achievement."*
— Golda Meir

On a separate piece of paper, or on the white space on this
page, make a list of all the things other people have ever
complimented you on or told you you were good at. Also
include things you yourself think you just might
have a knack or passion for.

These are your inner sparks of possibility. Now how can you
fan them into flames of achievement?

Circle one or two you want to work on today. Then put down
this book and go do something that fans the flame.
Keep fanning until it ignites.

*I am making the most of my life by fanning my tiny, inner
sparks of possibility into flames of achievement.*

# JUNE 2

*"And the day came when the risk to remain tight in the bud was more painful than the risk it took to blossom."*

— Anaïs Nin

Imagine yourself as a rosebush in bud. Each bud is one or your passions, dreams, or audacious goals.

How many of your buds have already burst into bloom? How many remain tight in the bud?

This book is about three things: Appreciating the blooms, mourning the blooms that have faded, and focusing awareness on the buds. All three require our mindful attention. One will naturally overshadow the others on any given day.

On days when we are feeling a particular bud most strongly, it is time to mindfully give it a little extra sun, water, and fertilizer. It is time to coax it into bloom.

*The buds of my passions, dreams, and audacious goals deserve my awareness and attention.*

# JUNE 3

*"Many persons have a wrong idea of what constitutes true happiness.
It is not attained through self-gratification but through
fidelity to a worthy purpose."*

— Helen Keller

Self-indulgence is overrated.

Oh sure, sensual pleasures and immersive recreation are fun,
but they're ephemeral. They're strictly "in the now." Only when
we add intention, values, and a sense of purpose to the
now do we get meaning.

True happiness is more about making meaning than making
merry. What's the cure for unhappiness, then? Not fun but
pursuing purpose. A helpful distinction for us to keep in mind.

*My happiness is tied to spending my time on
things I find meaningful.*

# JUNE 4

*"If you get tired, learn to rest—not to quit."*

— Author Unknown

Fatigue is a symptom. When we're tired—physically, cognitively, emotionally, socially, or spiritually—we need rest.

Mindfulness is about paying attention to our inner truths. When we're aware of how we're feeling, we can take care of ourselves appropriately. Fatigue usually means we need to turn further inward for a while to recenter and lavish ourselves with self-care.

Rest is essential. The more wise (ahem, older) I become, the more I understand the necessity of respite and recuperation. I sometimes take a few weeks of rest at a time. I'm not quitting— and neither should you. Instead, I'm gathering and refilling myself so that I can once again effectively act in the world.

*When I get tired, I will rest—not quit.*

# JUNE 5

*"As you walk and eat and travel, be where you are.*
*Otherwise you will miss most of your life."*

— Buddha

Be here, I tell myself,
but soon my mind runs away.

Be here, I say again,
returning my mind to the now.

Be here. Be here. Be here.

It's a mantra worth repeating
as often as we need to.

*Be here, I tell myself in the now. Be here,*
*I repeat. Be here. Be here. Be here.*

# JUNE 6

*"Finally, brothers and sisters, whatever is true, whatever is noble,*
*whatever is right, whatever is pure, whatever is lovely,*
*whatever is admirable—if anything is excellent or*
*praiseworthy—think about such things and the*
*God of peace will be with you."*

— Philippians 4:8

What, to you, is true, noble, right, pure, lovely, admirable, excellent, or praiseworthy? I believe that it is these things that align with your purpose and feed your divine spark.

Mindfully structuring your day to spend as much time as possible in the presence of the things and beings that fit one or more of these criteria will improve the quality of your life.

For today, pick just one of the adjectives. What to you, for instance, is admirable? How can you inject your day with at least a small dose of this? Here are a few ideas: Write a note to someone you admire telling them why. Read a book or watch a biopic about someone you admire. Practice an activity you admire, even if you're just a beginner. Reach out to a mentor who can teach you more about the thing you admire.

*I will mindfully incorporate things that are true, noble, right,*
*pure, lovely, admirable, excellent, and praiseworthy into my life.*

# JUNE 7

*"This body, too: Such is its nature, such is its future,*
*such its unavoidable fate."*

— The Kāyagatā sati Sutta

Some Buddhist monks spend time contemplating corpses in
various stages of decay. The practice is believed to help the
monks conquer fear, transcend thought,
and achieve pure awareness.

Thinking about the eventual death of our bodies may be scary
for most of us, but as my many funeral director friends will tell
you, death is as normal and natural as life. Befriending the idea
of our own deaths cannot only help us grow more comfortable
with death, it can also help us live more deeply.

Our bodies will one day be stilled by death. What happens after
that? I'm not sure, but I do believe we go on somehow.
I am sure, however, that until that day arrives,
we have lots of real living—not just existing—to do.

*I want to truly live until I die.*

# JUNE 8

*"Failure is simply the opportunity to begin again,*
*this time more intelligently."*

— Henry Ford

Do you remember learning how to ride a bike? I do. I remember
tipping over. I remember that sickening wobbly feeling. But I
also remember that click of my body's balancing system
telling me, "Oh! I see how this works!"

Pretty much everything we do in life follows this same pattern.
We try. We fail. We get better. We wobble less. Only over time
and with lots of practice do we gain mastery.

Let's not be afraid of failure. Failure is simply evidence that we're
acting in the world. Everyone falls when they're first
learning to ride a bike—except for the people who
never try to learn how to ride a bike.

*When I fail, I will remember that my failure is simply an*
*opportunity to begin again, this time more intelligently.*

# JUNE 9

*"Death is the sound of distant thunder at a picnic."*

— W.H. Auden

In this book's Introduction, I talked about death awareness and how incorporating it into your daily life can transform your capacity for living in the now. Today I want to bring us back to this essential principle.

Each of us will die. Maybe some of us will even die yet this month or this year.

Is that a morbid thought? I don't think so. It's just the truth. In fact, the belief that death awareness and death talk are morbid is evidence that our culture has death all wrong.

Dedicating a few moments every day to considering our eventual deaths helps us live more fully all the other moments of each day. So let's imagine the day of our death for a minute. Got it? Now reflect on what that image helps you understand about today.

*Mindful awareness of my own eventual death helps me live more fully today.*

# JUNE 10

*"Say yes to the situations that stretch you and scare you and ask you to be a better you than you think you can be."*

— Annie Downs

Act. Do. Move. Go.

In this book, I'm encouraging you to mindfully pursue your passions and relish the now. But busyness is not the goal. Doing can also be mindless. So how do you tell which actions are mindless and which are mindful?

One way is to ask yourself if you're saying yes to actions that stretch you and scare you and ask you to be a better you than you think you can be. Actions that are the opposite—overly rote and perhaps even self-demeaning—are often things better left by the wayside.

Say yes to learning, growth, and fulfillment.

*I say yes to situations that stretch me and scare me and ask me to be a better me that I think I can be.*

# JUNE 11

*"The greatest happiness of life is the conviction that we are loved—
loved for ourselves, or rather, loved in spite of ourselves."*

— Victor Hugo

Staying present to the love in our lives is a challenge for those of
us who are uncomfortable with vulnerability and imperfection.
To acknowledge and accept the love of others is to admit that
we are worthy and so are they—even though it's so
obvious that we both are imperfect.

How do you behave when someone expresses their love for
you? Do you tend to wave it off, or do you soak it in? Reveling
in a moment of love and affection is living in the now.

Mindfully embracing love means ignoring the chatter of our
judgmental, distractable egos and instead luxuriating in every
moment of tenderness. Love here now.

*To live in the now is to love in the now.*

# JUNE 12

*"The moment one gives close attention to anything, even a blade of grass, it becomes a mysterious, awesome, indescribably magnificent world in itself."*

— Henry Miller

Our modern lives are so overloaded with sensory data that it's become increasingly hard for us to focus on one single thing.

Look around you. How many manmade objects are within seeing distance? Hundreds? Thousands? And if you were to pick up your phone, tablet, or computer, how many videos, songs, memes, photos, ideas, and words would you have at your fingertips? Untold trillions.

Venturing out into nature is one way to find magnificence again. Another is to clear a space in your home—perhaps your bedroom or a spare room or a patio area—of anything you don't absolutely need or love. Get rid of every single piece of clutter. Aim for monk-like spareness. Then when you're in nature or your serene space (no technology allowed!), you'll be ready to give close attention to a single object and see that it is a mysterious, awesome, indescribably magnificent world unto itself.

*Each thing and being is a mysterious, awesome, indescribably magnificent world in itself.*

# JUNE 13

*"You are growing into consciousness, and my wish for you is
that you feel no need to constrict yourself to
make other people comfortable."*

— Ta-Nehisi Coates

This is something I have seen happen in my own life as well
as in the lives of friends and those I have had the honor of
counseling. As we grow more mindful, we may begin to awaken
to truths that reveal old habits and patterns to be
limiting or even destructive.

We grow and we change. The people and situations around us
may not. They are often not comfortable with our growth. They
may perceive the changes in us as undesirable or false when in
fact they are deeply genuine.

Do not constrict yourself to make other people comfortable.
Become fully yourself. You cannot control how others will
respond to your heightened consciousness. All you can do is be
kind and understanding as you keep on growing.

*Even when it makes other people uncomfortable, I will not
restrict myself as I grow into consciousness.*

# JUNE 14

*"Everyone thinks of changing the world, but no one thinks of changing himself."*

— Leo Tolstoy

As I write this, the United States is in political chaos. People are deeply divided, and leaders are not living up to expectations.

We want things to change, and we often share our opinions about how they should change. But the mindful approach to all of this is to start with ourselves.

A good question is: What are my values? When we've identified our values, we can then ask ourselves: How am I living my values? This very day, how will I affirm my values?

The world will only change when people change. And people in general will only change when individuals change. Let's mindfully begin with ourselves.

*When I want to change the world,*
*I will remember to start with myself.*

# JUNE 15

*"All you need is love. But a little chocolate now
and then doesn't hurt."*

— Charles Schulz

Charles Schulz, the Peanuts comic strip cartoonist, also famously said that happiness is a warm puppy.

We get little bursts of happy brain chemicals—such as dopamine, oxytocin, GABA, and endorphins—from living in the now. For example, dopamine is released when we achieve a goal. So, working in the present toward a future reality makes us feel good in the now. Oxytocin is released through physical contact with a loved one or companion animal. When we snuggle with a warm puppy, we feel good in the now.

GABA, which creates a feeling of calmness, is released during yoga and meditation, and endorphins are released during exercise and sex.

And chocolate? Our brains love chocolate because it causes the release of more than 300 biochemical compounds in our bodies, including tryptophan and serotonin, which enhance feelings of relaxation and wellbeing.

Today, let's mindfully choose activities and treats that make our now more pleasurable.

*I mindfully choose activities and treats that make
my now more pleasurable.*

# JUNE 16

*"With every experience, you alone are painting your own canvas,
thought by thought, choice by choice."*

— Oprah Winfrey

Wait a sec. I'm not painting my own canvas. Every day my life is
affected by circumstances and realities outside my control.

This is true. But! (You knew there was a "but" coming, right?)
Only I decide how to respond to the circumstances and realities.
Only I set my intention to make choices that will
take me where I want to go next.

My canvas may be a mess, but it's *my* mess, and it's beautiful. I
choose to see it that way. I choose to seek out more of the parts
that feel like fulfilling my purpose. When challenges come
along, I choose to embrace them and open myself to
what I can learn from them.

I *am* painting my own canvas. So are you. How's it lookin'?

*I am painting my own canvas, thought by thought,
choice by choice.*

# JUNE 17

*"When is the last time that you had a great conversation, a
conversation that wasn't just two intersecting monologues, which
is what passes for conversation a lot in this culture? But…a great
conversation, in which you overheard yourself saying things that
you never knew you knew? That you heard yourself receiving from
somebody words that absolutely found places within you that you
thought you had lost…a conversation that brought the two
of you on to a different plane? …a conversation that continued to sing
in your mind for weeks afterwards…I've had some of them recently.
They are food and drink for the soul."*

— John O'Donohue

A great conversation is mindful communion among two or
more people. Important thoughts and feelings are shared.
Hearts are open. Long-festering griefs and secrets may be freed.

Think about the most important conversations you've
ever had in your life. Why were they so important?
What did they teach you?

Now think about someone you've been meaning to speak
with about something meaningful to you. Go arrange a great
conversation with this person today, before it's too late.

*I mindfully make time for and open my
heart to great conversations.*

# JUNE 18

*"Hope is being able to see that there is light
despite all of the darkness."*

— Desmond Tutu

Perhaps the main challenge of human existence is that we are self-aware, which means we are conscious of our pasts, presents, and potential futures all at the same time. That's why living in the now is so darned hard. Our brains are built to think outside the bounds of the present moment.

When we experience something difficult in life, we continue to think about and feel the pain of it long after the event is over. It is normal and necessary for us to acknowledge, feel, and express our grief. Our self-awareness forces us to befriend the darkness.

But even in the darkness, we must also cultivate hope. Our practice of living in the now helps us see that each day also presents us with opportunities for joy and gratitude. And in addition to prolonging pain, our self-awareness also acknowledges that our lives have been good and can be good again.

There is darkness, and there is light. Human life is a beautiful, dappled blend of both.

*When I consider my past, present, and future,
I know that there is light despite all of the darkness.*

# JUNE 19

*"Omnipotence is not knowing how everything is done; it's just doing it."*

— Alan Watts

Too often, what stops us from mindfully pursuing our goals is a lack of understanding of how to move forward. We're here, our goal's way over there, and we don't know how to effectively get from here to there.

But here's the thing: We don't need to know in advance *how* to do something. We just need to *do* and learn as we go.

I'm not advocating foolhardiness, but I am encouraging action. If you're stuck on a life goal or desire, for goodness sake, do something about it! It's OK if you don't know how it's done. That's part of the adventure.

Just take one tiny step today. Tomorrow you can take another tiny step. And when you mess up? No biggie. Just make a course correction and keep going.

*I don't have to know in advance how things are done. I just have to begin doing them.*

# JUNE 20

*"The place to be happy is here. The time to be happy is now."*
— Robert G. Ingersoll

In June in Colorado, which is where I live, yellow swallowtail butterflies can be seen flitting from flower to flower and garden to garden. They're so lovely. What a delight to stand back and watch them fly and swoop, pause to eat, and fan their wings.

Whenever I'm struggling with mindless worry or stress, I would be well-served to remember the swallowtail. Life is beautiful. Like a butterfly, I have the privilege of flitting from pleasure to pleasure, activity to activity, person to person. Each of them are miraculous in their own ways, and if I choose to, I have the capacity to recognize and appreciate this in the now, as each encounter unfolds.

Off I go.

*Here is the place to be happy. Now is the time to be happy.*

# JUNE 21

*"Real devotion is an unbroken receptivity to the truth. Real devotion is rooted in an awed and reverent gratitude, but one that is lucid, grounded, and intelligent."*

—Sogyal Rinpoche

I've known a number of people in my life who embodied the "don't worry, be happy" mantra. They seemed to live in the moment and were always quick to laugh and find ways to enjoy themselves. Wonderful, right?

The more I was present to these people, though, the more I realized that some of them were only living in the "good" moments. They constantly sought happiness and actively worked to deny, ignore, or minimize loss, sadness, boredom, disappointment, anger, and other normal and necessary but challenging emotions.

Mindful living requires awareness of the truth in each moment. We're not living in the now if we're not fully, honestly experiencing our inner and outer realities.

Don't worry. Be whatever this moment calls upon you to be.

---

*I mindfully inhabit the truth of each moment.*
*I don't try to skip the bad parts.*

# JUNE 22

*"We might begin by scanning our body . . . and then asking,
'What is happening?' We might also ask, 'What wants my attention
right now?' or, 'What is asking for acceptance?'"*

— Tara Brach

Let's get mindful right now. As psychologist and spiritual guru
Tara Brach suggests, we can begin by scanning our bodies.

What do we feel in our bodies? Right now my arms are a bit
cold, and my eyes are tired. I also notice that I'm slouching,
so I'm going to sit up.

What wants my attention right now? Am I feeling something
emotionally or spiritually that wants me to be aware of it?
Actually, now that I consider this, I can sense a pull
toward one of my children. Maybe it has something to
do with a conversation we had yesterday.
I'll call her after I finish this entry.

What is asking for my acceptance? I need a few more meditative
minutes to embrace that question.

How about you? What is happening with your body?
What wants your attention? What is asking for your acceptance?
You'll find the answers in your now.

*What is happening with my body? What wants my
attention? What is asking for my acceptance?
I'll find the answers in the now.*

# JUNE 23

*"It's smart to question whether we should always be living in the moment. The latest research on imagination and creativity shows that if we're always in the moment, we're going to miss out on important connections between our own inner mind-wandering thoughts and the outside world. Creativity lies in that intersection between our outer world and our inner world."*

— Scott Barry Kaufman

You know who always, always lives in the now? My dogs. I've had numerous beloved companion canines over the years. My current furry children are Zoey and Laney, both Puggles—a Beagle/Pug mix. Without fail, all of my dogs—and all dogs in general, of course—have been more fully aware of the present moment than I could ever hope to be.

Dogs, however, lack mindfulness. Mindfulness is applying intention to the now. When we take breaks from the now that is outside of us to pay attention to the now that is inside of us, we create space for our souls to speak. Meditation is one way of accomplishing this. Daydreaming is another.

Inward awareness is just as important as outward awareness. I hope you'll join me in trying to find that balance.

*I mindfully seek a balance between inward awareness and outward awareness.*

# JUNE 24

*"Everyone should have a sense of urgency. It is getting a lot done in a short period of time in a calm, confident manner."*

— Bob Proctor

Money isn't our most limited resource. Time is. We can find ways to make more money if we need it, but we can't manufacture more time.

Mindfulness is about making the most of the precious time we have. First, we're present in the now, so we're aware of and experiencing each moment. And second, we're conscious of spending our time as much as possible on the people and activities we value most.

I agree: Everyone should have a sense of urgency. Let's proceed calmly and confidently into this day and remember that time is precious.

*I will proceed calmly and confidently into this day and remember that time is precious.*

# JUNE 25

*"The hardest thing to listen to—your instinct, your personal human intuition—always whispers; it never shouts."*
— Stephen Spielberg

When we make time for quiet stillness each day, whether we are meditating or simply stopping to just "be" and observe the world around us, we create the opportunity for our quiet inner knowing to be heard.

In the hustle and bustle of our everyday lives, it can be a challenge for us to notice what our intuition is trying to tell us. It often whispers, and if we're not training our awareness on that whisper, we run the risk of missing it altogether.

The good news is that the more we listen for the whisper of our soul, the better we get at hearing it, and the more we are able to apply its wisdom to the now each day.

What is your intuition telling you today? Shhh…
Quiet yourself and really listen.

*I will quiet myself so I can hear the whisper of my intuition.*

# JUNE 26

*"I am learning slowly to bring my crazy pinball-machine mind back to this place of friendly detachment toward myself, so I can look out at the world and see all those other things with respect. Try looking at your mind as a wayward puppy that you are trying to paper train. You don't drop-kick a puppy into the neighbor's yard every time it piddles on the floor. You just keep bringing it back to the newspaper. So I keep trying gently to bring my mind back to what is really there to be seen, maybe to be seen and noted with a kind of reverence."*

— Anne Lamott

Paper training a puppy—that's a good analogy for the beginner's mindfulness practice. Our minds are puppies, constantly leaping and running and frisking from one interesting stimulus or thought to the next.

But like puppies, our minds can be trained. We can return them to the present or to our breath over and over again, until they're more likely to rest there automatically.

There's a lot to see, respect, and revere in the now, but only if we muster the daily diligence to train our puppy minds. And that's what we're doing together on these pages.

---

*I am paper-training my puppy mind, over and over and over.*

# JUNE 27

*"To be born is to be chosen."*

— John O'Donohue

Maybe we're not good enough.

Maybe we make terrible choices. Maybe we've done some bad things. Maybe other people are more deserving of the good things in life than we are.

Horsefeathers. If you were born, you were chosen. You're perfectly imperfect, just like every other human being who's ever walked the earth.

Mindfulness and kindness are the two essential practices that allow us to be the best we can be. And really, kindness is a natural consequence of mindfulness, because when we are mindful and observing of our own egos, we understand that kindness is the highest value.

You were chosen, and now you must only choose to be mindful.

*I am here, so I was chosen. Now I choose to pay homage to my chosenness by living fully and mindfully in the now.*

# JUNE 28

*"Integrity is choosing courage over comfort. It's choosing what is right over what is fun, fast, or easy. It's choosing to practice your values rather than simply professing them."*

— Dr. Brené Brown

What are your values? List the top five right now.

In what ways have you lived your values today? Mindfulness requires us to connect our inner truths with our outward living. We become aware of what is really, truly important to us and why we are here, then we carry out that awareness as we go about our daily lives.

Fun, fast, and easy are often (but not always) mindless. Efficient is often not effective. Let's mindfully incorporate activities into each day that help us practice our values. It's these very activities that ultimately give us a sense of meaning and purpose.

*I choose what is right over what is fun, fast, or easy.*

# JUNE 29

*"A flower does not think of competing with the flower next to it.*
*It just blooms."*

— Zen Shin

Our egos like to compare ourselves with others. Are we more or less attractive than that person? Wealthier or poorer? Smarter or dumber? More or less talented? More or less successful?

When we mindfully work to ignore our egos' need to compare, we begin to let go of both self-doubt and hubris. We're not less than or better than. We're just who we are.

Instead of thinking of life as a competition, let's think of it as a meadow carpeted with a riot of wildflowers. In being fully present to our lives, each of us blooms uniquely and gloriously. How wonderful each of us is.

*I bloom like a single flower in a meadow full of wildflowers.*
*How wonderful each of us is.*

# JUNE 30

*"The miracle is not to walk on water. The miracle is to walk on the green earth, dwelling deeply in the present moment, feeling fully alive."*

— Thich Nhat Hanh

Are you a believer in a miracles? I am. I'm open to the mystery of amazing things that happen that are beyond the realm of our mortal understanding.

But the more mindful we become, the more we realize that the happenings we typically call "miracles" are no more miraculous, really, than what we are privileged to experience when we are fully present in our everyday lives.

This ladybug walking across my desk? A miracle. My wife's laugh and my children's uniquely beautiful ways of being? Miracles. The Colorado mountains outside my window? Miracles.

I challenge you to notice at least ten everyday miracles today. When you spot them, stop and express your gratitude in some way.

*I will be on the watch for everyday miracles today.*

# JULY 1

*"Walk as if you are kissing the earth with your feet."*
— Thich Nhat Hanh

This earth of ours is a miraculous home. Every step we are privileged to take on its surface is a gift.

Walking meditation is an effective mindfulness practice for many. In lieu of training our awareness on our breath, we might try training it on our step. As we walk, we feel the bottoms of our feet make contact with the ground. We feel the roll of our foot from heel to toe.

With each step, we are saying thank you. Thank you, earth, for supporting us with your resources. Thank you for your shelter. Thank you for your beauty. We mindfully walk, and we express our gratitude.

*Today as I walk, I will be mindful of my gratitude for this earth.*

# JULY 2

*"The hardest battle you're ever going to fight is the battle to just be you."*

— Leo Buscaglia

It takes many of us a long time to figure out who we really are.

There's so much cultural pressure to conform. We grow up believing we have to look a certain way, act a certain way, follow a certain path. Everything outside of us has pressured us to fit into a certain box.

But now we're looking at it from the opposite direction. We're working on living from the inside out instead of the other way around. We're getting to know our divine sparks and our unique purposes. We're on a mission to acquaint ourselves with our own souls.

The authentic you, in the now. That is everything.

*I am living from the inside out instead of the other way around.*

# JULY 3

*"The way to live in the present is to remember that 'This too shall pass.' When you experience joy, remembering that 'This too shall pass' helps you savor the here and now. When you experience pain and sorrow, remembering that 'This too shall pass' reminds you that grief, like joy, is only temporary."*

— Joey Green

Life is change. Everything is temporary.

Well, everything but love. Some love lasts forever. Which means, of course, that the grief that results from love also lasts forever. So I have to take issue with Joey Green there. Everything but love and grief are temporary.

When we mindfully encounter a challenge, we experience it fully in the now. We befriend it. But we can also remind ourselves that since change is a constant in human life, the challenge is temporary. This too shall pass.

Unless it's true love, or its conjoined twin, grief. Those it is our privilege to hold in our hearts always.

---

*This too shall pass—unless it is true love or its conjoined twin, grief. Those it is my privilege to hold in my heart always.*

# JULY 4

*"These are the times in which a genius would wish to live. It is not in the still calm of life, or the repose of a pacific station, that great characters are formed. The habits of a vigorous mind are formed in contending with difficulties. Great necessities call out great virtues. When a mind is raised, and animated by scenes that engage the heart, then those qualities which would otherwise lay dormant, wake into life and form the character of the hero and the statesman."*

— Abigail Adams

In one way or another, hard times befall most of us. And it is in the crucible of loss and challenge that our characters are formed.

At each moment we have a choice: to look fully and openly at life, or to close our eyes and do our best to suppress, ignore, or deny our potential to positively respond to hardship.

Our forbearers rose to the challenge. Their consciousnesses were raised. Their hearts were awakened. They mindfully, intentionally, became heroes and statespeople.

Which great necessities in your life are calling out to your great virtues? How will you respond?

---

*Great necessities call out great virtues.*
*I am gathering myself to respond.*

# JULY 5

*"The real voyage of discovery consists not in seeking new landscapes but in having new eyes."*

— Marcel Proust

Scientific studies have shown that while adults are better than young children at focusing on certain stimuli in their environments, young children are better at noticing random details.

As we grow up, we learn to pay attention to what we've been told is important. But what if other things going on around us are actually *more* important than the so-called important things we've been paying attention to all along?

Learning to see with new eyes is challenging. We can make it a game, though. When we are in a familiar place and we're trying to be mindful, we can ask ourselves to look for ten new things. We can scan the room or environment for ten objects, people, sounds, smells, or tactile sensations we've never really noticed before. Look and count: 1, 2, 3, 4, 5, 6, 7, 8, 9, 10.

*I can learn to see with new eyes by training my awareness on that which I've never really paid attention to before.*

# JULY 6

*"A perfect summer day is when the sun is shining, the breeze is blowing, the birds are singing, and the lawn mower is broken."*

— James Dent

To appreciate a summer's day is to be present to it. Especially in the summer, I try to carve out time to simply be. I block off my calendar for several intermittent weeks of intentional sloth.

Still, there's always something that needs doing. Even on my vacation days, there are errands to run, appointments to keep, emails to answer, and chores to do.

Or are there? On some days of our choosing, why can't we set aside anything that feels like an obligation? Why can't we block out entire days or weeks to wholly vacate our normal lives and simply and truly live in the now?

We can, of course. We just have to recognize that we can and should.

*There's always something that needs doing, but I don't always need to be doing something.*

# JULY 7

*"We are always getting ready to live but never living."*
— Ralph Waldo Emerson

How much of today will you spend getting
ready to do something else?

We get ready for the day by grooming, dressing, eating
breakfast, perhaps driving to work. We might get ready for a
meeting by reviewing paperwork, and maybe we get ready for
dinner by Googling recipes and stopping by the grocery store.
We get ready to pay bills, take a vacation, start a diet,
and go to sleep. We get ready to start school,
find a partner, have children, and retire.

The take-away is this: The getting-ready part is just as much
living as the what-we're-getting-ready-for part.

Life is always now. All of it counts. All of it is precious. Every
minute of it is ours to relish or to overlook. The choice is ours.

*Getting ready for something still counts as living.
Life is always now.*

# JULY 8

*"It does not matter how long you are spending on the earth, how much money you have gathered, or how much attention you have received. It is the amount of positive vibration you have radiated in life that matters."*

— Amit Ray

Human cells vibrate. On a subatomic level, the molecules that comprise them are in constant motion. Some people believe that the higher the frequency of the vibration, the more health, happiness, and enlightenment you will attain.

You raise your vibrational frequency through mindfulness. All of the daily meditations in this book help. Practices like naming gratitudes, spending time in nature, eating healthfully, exercising your body, and meditating all help.

The idea is that when you radiate positive vibrations, not only are you more authentic and joyful, but you promote authenticity and joy in others as well. It's as if you send ripples of your own energy out into the world. Imagine if everyone rippled mindfully with positive intentions.

*I seek to vibrate at ever-higher frequencies.*

# JULY 9

*"Generosity is another quality which, like patience, letting go, non-judging, and trust, provides a solid foundation for mindfulness practice. You might experiment with using the cultivation of generosity as a vehicle for deep self-observation and inquiry as well as an exercise in giving. A good place to start is with yourself. See if you can give yourself gifts that may be true blessings, such as self-acceptance, or some time each day with no purpose. Practice feeling deserving enough to accept these gifts without obligation—to simply receive from yourself, and from the universe."*

— John Kabat-Zinn

Are you generous toward yourself? Most of us aren't. Most of us spend more time, money, and effort giving to others than we do to ourselves.

Service to others gives life meaning. I believe that. But I also know that each of us is also deserving of self-care. After all, mindfulness and living in the now are practices meant to enhance our quality of life. We start with ourselves in each moment and work outward from there.

How can you be generous with yourself today? Be on the lookout for opportunities.

*Today I will be generous with myself and know that I am deserving.*

# JULY 10

*"Real love amounts to withholding the truth, even when you're offered the perfect opportunity to hurt someone's feelings."*

— David Sedaris

The truth isn't always mindful. Hewing to it too rigidly often leads to pain and injustice.

Rotary Club members ascribe to a moral code they call the "Four-Way Test." Before they speak or act, they ask themselves four things:

1. Is it the truth?

2. Is it fair to all concerned?

3. Will it build goodwill and better friendships?

4. Will it be beneficial to all concerned?

Only when a possible comment or action meets all four parts of the test is it considered useful. Note that "the truth" is just one of the four criteria.

Let's remember to be mindful of our broader goals and intentions. The Four-Way Test is an effective tool in the now.

---

*I can use the Four-Way Test to help me speak mindfully in the now.*

# JULY 11

*"Come back to square one, just the minimum bare bones. Relaxing with the present moment, relaxing with hopelessness, relaxing with death, not resisting the fact that things end, that things pass, that things have no lasting substance, that everything is changing all the time—that is the basic message."*

— Pema Chödrön

Some days we just need to come back to square one.

Some days all we can manage is the minimum bare bones. Breathe, exist, sleep if we're lucky.

Life can be really hard, and when it is, our mindfulness practice can sustain us. We can live in the now with our hopelessness. We can live in the now with our pain. We can live in the now with our lack of control. We can live in the now with the ravages of constant change.

If we can manage mindfulness in these circumstances, we will find that we can bear witness to our own pain. There is the hurt, and then there is our eternal consciousness observing the hurt. It is this consciousness that understands that the pain is temporary and mortal life an illusion.

*Some days I just need to come back to square one.*

# JULY 12

*"Sunsets are so beautiful they almost seem as if we were looking through the gates of heaven."*

— John Lubbock

Watching the sun set is a mindfulness activity.

It's a way to anchor ourselves to the beauty of the here and now. We marvel at the colors and at the composition of the clouds and the horizon. We feel awe and gratitude. We are often able to dismiss other thoughts from our minds and simply witness and feel.

Watch the sun set (or rise) today or tomorrow if you can. Could you also take the next step and incorporate sunset-gazing into your daily practice? If not, what similar activity could you substitute?

*Witnessing nature helps anchor me to the beauty of the here and now.*

# JULY 13

*"The things we think about, brood on, dwell on, and exult over influence our life in a thousand ways. When we can actually choose the direction of our thoughts instead of just letting them run along the grooves of conditioned thinking, we become the masters of our own lives."*

— Eknath Easwaran

Which thoughts do you tend to think over and over again? Which responses in you are largely automatic?

Most of us live our lives under the control of conditioned thinking. And it's so fundamental to our thoughts and responses that we mistake it for truth or "just the way things are." We don't realize we've been brainwashed.

We must learn to be aware of our own assumptions. For example, I was raised to believe that everyone should work hard to earn the life they want. But what if the virtues of hard work are, at least in part, a myth? What if, as many spiritual gurus believe, ease and grace are the better path?

Today, every time we catch ourselves in a conditioned thought or response, let's ask ourselves why. Why do we think or act that way? Would a different thought or response serve us— and the world—better?

*I will examine my conditioned thinking and choose new thoughts that serve me and the world.*

# JULY 14

*"It is not enough to be busy. The question is:*
*What are we busy about?"*

— Henry David Thoreau

I'm getting to the point in my life where I'm finally wise enough to have a healthy disdain for busyness. I don't want to be so busy anymore! I've learned, at long last, that just as efficient is not the same as effective, busy is not the same as productive. When you're overly busy, though, sometimes it's hard to know what and where to begin trimming. What is effective, productive, meaningful activity, and what is merely mindless time-wasting?

Thoreau is famous for his experiment in simple living, which he undertook in 1845 on a piece of rural property owned by Ralph Waldo Emerson on the shore of Walden Pond, in Massachusetts. He built himself a one-room cabin there and lived off the land. "I went to the woods to live deliberately," he wrote.

I too find that spending time in nature helps me sort out what is essential and what is not. After a day spent hiking in the mountains or walking a desert trail, I am much more attuned to the still, small voice inside of me. Give it a try. Take a mental health day soon and enjoy it mindfully, un-busily, in the outdoors. It will help you sort out how to un-busy the rest of your days.

*Busyness is not a virtue. I am learning to choose activities mindfully.*

# JULY 15

*"These are the days that must happen to you."*

— Walt Whitman

Do you believe in the concept of destiny?

I think that each of us has unique gifts and purposes to fulfill here on earth, but I don't believe our lives are preordained. It's up to us to find our way and choose to live with as much love and meaning as possible, no matter what happens.

Along the way, we will encounter certain days that must happen to us. Things necessarily change. Rites of passage unfold. Children grow up. Parents die. We age. There is no avoiding loss and grief.

On these days (and there are many), the question becomes: How will I live mindfully, in the now, on the days that must happen to me? Together we are seeking the answer.

*On the days that must happen to me,*
*I will be present and mindful.*

# JULY 16

*"You cannot let a fear of failure, or a fear of comparison, or a fear of judgment, stop you from doing what's going to make you great. I don't think you should do just what makes you happy. I think you should do what makes you great."*

— Charlie Day

On the one hand, happy. On the other hand, great.

It's easier to pursue happiness, right? Hanging out with friends and family, good food, good drink, a little entertainment, simple treats and pleasures. Every day we're presented with opportunities for bursts of happiness. Living in the now demands that we say yes to these, at least some of the time.

But greatness, that we have to work for. It often takes years of learning and effort, trial and error, to achieve greatness at something. The daily grind of it isn't necessarily fun or "happy," thought it should be sprinkled with fun and happiness, at least now and then.

I agree with Charlie. I think you should do what makes you great. By all means, get daily doses of happy, but dedicate a chunk of each day to the pursuit of greatness too. You'll be so glad you did.

---

*I will do what makes me great.*

# JULY 17

*"You must expect great things of yourself*
*before you can do them."*

— Michael Jordan

Ah, the power of intention.

But first, desire. We start from a place of stillness, listening for
the whisper of our souls. What is it telling us it wants? What
does it yearn for? What does it need?

Then we mindfully declare our intention to carry out the desires
of our souls. We move from saying
"I want…" to saying "I will…"

If we are committed to acting in the now, each day, to fulfill our
intentions, we begin to expect things of ourselves.

Desire. Intention. Action. Expectation.

*I desire. I intend. I act. I expect.*

# JULY 18

*"Live today. Not yesterday. Not tomorrow. Just today.
Inhabit your moments. Don't rent them out to tomorrow. Do you
know what you're doing when you spend a moment wondering
how things are going to turn out? You're cheating yourself out
of today. Today is calling to you, trying to get your attention,
but you're stuck on tomorrow, and today trickles away
like water down a drain. You wake up the next morning and
that today you wasted is gone forever. It's now yesterday.
Some of those moments may have had wonderful things
in store for you, but now you'll never know."*

— Jerry Spinelli

What if today you were given a pot of money that you could
only spend today? Use it or lose it.

You'd spend it, right? You'd find a way to blow it. And if you
received a new pot of money each day, you'd experiment for a
while, but you'd soon figure out the most effective, meaningful
ways to spend it down each day.

Time, of course, is more valuable than money.
So have you found the most effective, meaningful
ways to spend today, today?

---

*Each day I mindfully work to live this one day.*

# JULY 19

*"Don't believe everything you think.*
*Thoughts are just that—thoughts."*

— Allan Lokos

Funnily enough, mindfulness is largely about getting
out of our minds and into our bodies or our souls.

Think of your mind as a bossy administrative assistant. Its
organizational and analytical skills come in handy,
but it's a bit too self-important. And it tends to get
worked up about inconsequential things.

Our minds should serve the intentions and purposes of our
souls. They should also help our bodies stay well and enjoy life.
Educating and sharpening our minds is essential too, so that
they can better carry out their executive tasks.

But our minds are not our essence.
Let's think about that today.

*My mind is not my essence. I use my mind to help carry out the*
*intentions and purposes of my essence.*

# JULY 20

*"Treat everyone you meet as if they were you."*

— Doug Dillon

Empathy is the capacity to put yourself in someone else's shoes. It's the human quality that allows us to try to understand and experience what another person might be experiencing, given their unique circumstances.

That homeless guy on the street corner holding the cardboard sign? Imagine it's you who's holding the sign. What set of life predicaments could put you there? What advantages have you been given along the way that this person might not have?

Here's an even better way to enter the mindfulness of empathy: Treat everyone you meet as if they were your child. That homeless guy on the corner? He's your son. Now how do you respond to him?

Kindness and love are central to our mindfulness practice— self-kindness and self-love as well as kindness and love toward others. Everyone deserves them.

*I treat everyone I meet as if I am them.*

# JULY 21

*"Behold the turtle. He makes progress only when he sticks his neck out."*

— James B. Conant

Two questions: What do you care most about? And how often do you stick your neck out for these beloved people and things?

Sticking your neck out means taking a risk for something you think is important. It means making yourself vulnerable in exchange for upholding values or possible reward.

Yes, you have to take risks, big and little, day in and day out, to live your best life. Nothing ventured, nothing gained. You have to stick your neck out. How will you stick your neck out today?

*I make progress only when I stick my neck out.*

# JULY 22

*"If you want to change the world, start off by making your bed."*
— William H. McCraven

A U.S. Navy Admiral, McCraven says that making your bed every morning helps you start your day with a sense of accomplishment and pride.

It encourages you to do other little tasks, which in turn add up to big tasks. It also demonstrates that the small stuff matters. And when you come home at night to a made bed, you feel a sense of order and encouragement.

Making your bed takes just one minute, but it's a mindful use of time that can make a big difference in your day. If you're not a bed maker, I encourage you to give it a try. Stick with it for at least a couple of months, and notice how it changes you.

*I make my bed every morning because it's a mindful minute that sends ripples of good intention through the rest of my day.*

# JULY 23

*"True discipline is really just self-remembering;*
*no forcing or fighting is necessary."*

— Charles Eisenstein

Those of us who've relied on self-discipline to try to lose weight
know that in any given moment, our desire to enjoy the now
can easily overtake our longer-term goals.

I like this other way of thinking about self-discipline. Self-
remembering isn't about constraining ourselves.
Instead, it's about reminding ourselves of who we truly are.
It's about mindfully recalling our best intentions and truest
selves as much and as often as possible.

Self-remembering is, in fact, mindfulness. When we remember
who we are and we bring that genuine presence to each
moment, we don't have to worry or stress,
force or fight. We only have to *be*.

*When I remember who I am, it is easier to carry out*
*my intention in each moment.*

# JULY 24

*"Why not just live in the moment,*
*especially if it has a good beat?"*

— Goldie Hawn

Psychological studies show that people listen to music for two
main reasons: to change or guide their moods,
and to heighten self-awareness.

Huzzah! That means music is a mindfulness tool!

Music helps us experience our feelings in the now. It also helps
us understand ourselves. It facilitates thoughts and feelings
about who we are, who we would like to be,
and how we might get from here to there.

Listen to some music today that speaks to your soul. Also listen
to some music that lifts your mood. Notice how both affect your
mindfulness practice. Consider incorporating
more music into your days.

*Music helps me live in the moment.*

# JULY 25

*"Accepting death doesn't mean you won't be devastated when some-
one you love dies. It means you will be able to focus on your grief,
unburdened by bigger existential questions like, 'Why do people die?'
and 'Why is this happening to me?' Death isn't happening to you.
Death is happening to us all."*

— Caitlin Doughty

Death awareness helps us live more fully.

What is death? Why do people die? What happens after death?
When will I die? When will those I love die?

The more we explore such questions before we come to grief,
the more comfortable we will be with the fact of death when
it happens. No, no one is ever truly ready for the death of a
loved one. But befriending death in general prepares us for the
fullness of life.

Spiritual practices, reading spiritual texts, discussion groups,
journaling—these and other ways of befriending mortality are
an essential part of a mindful life.

*I am befriending death in general and my own
mortality in particular.*

# JULY 26

*"You have escaped the cage.*
*Your wings are stretched out. Now, fly."*
— Rumi

Sometimes when I think about mindfulness, I picture a flock of migrating birds in the sky.

These birds have an inner knowing that is taking them to a particular destination. They are not conscious of where they are going, yet they are going somewhere with purpose and intention just the same.

Along the way, the migrating birds live in the now. They feel the sun on their backs and the wind on their wings. They stop to eat, drink, and rest. They chatter with one another. They deal with challenges as they arise.

We too can live in the now while working on bigger goals with purpose and intention. We can live our earthly lives even as we fly.

*I can live my earthly life even as I fly.*

# JULY 27

*"What good is the warmth of summer without the cold of winter to give it sweetness?"*

— John Steinbeck

What if nothing bad ever happened in life?
Have you ever considered that?

What if every day was beautiful, and everyone always had good health, people who loved them, a nice place to live, abundant food and drink, and work they enjoyed? What if earth were a utopia? What if no one ever died? Imagine that for a moment.

In this scenario, would we be incessantly happy? I don't think so. I think we need the bad to be able to appreciate the good. I believe we need the darkness to be able to bask in the light. I also think we need the unknown—the mystery—to have gratitude for the real in the now.

Human life presents us with contrasts. The yin and the yang are both necessary to form the whole. Let's work to be present to all of it.

*I need the darkness to be able to bask in the light.*

# JULY 28

*"To diminish the suffering of pain, we need to make a crucial distinction between the pain of pain, and the pain we create by our thoughts about the pain."*

— Howard Cutler

Usually when fear and worry are dominating our lives, it's because we're suffering from "dirty pain."

"Clean pain" is the normal pain that follows difficult life experiences. "Dirty pain" is the damaging, multiplied pain we create when we catastrophize, judge ourselves, or allow ourselves to be judged by others. Dirty pain is the story we tell ourselves about the clean pain. Dirty pain is the imaginary obstacles we put in our own way.

We can banish imaginary obstacles by mindfully, intentionally poking at them, though. Instead of continuing to speculate or assuming, we can find out the truth. We can ask. We can discuss with loved ones or a counselor. We can hold them up to the clear light of day.

When we poke our dirty fears, they often pop and vanish, leaving us with the healing presence of clean pain.

*I will be mindful of my dirty pain and banish it.*

# JULY 29

*"Rest is not idleness, and to lie sometimes on the grass under the*
*trees on a summer's day, listening to the murmur of water,*
*or watching clouds float across the blue sky,*
*is by no means a waste of time."*

— John Lubbock

Our common goal to live in the now sometimes feels at odds
with our common goal to mindfully use our time.

The mindful use of time often requires action. It asks us to take
steps each day toward fulfilling our purposes. However, after we
have been active for a time—physically, cognitively, emotionally,
socially, or spiritually—we need to rest. We need to rest our
weary bodies, minds, emotions, social selves, and souls.

Such rest recharges us. It is not idleness. It is not a waste of
time. Rather, it is an intentional, mindful way to live in the
now when our batteries are low.

*When I need it, rest is not idleness. It is an intentional, mindful*
*way to live in the now when my batteries are low.*

# JULY 30

*"Find out who you are and do it on purpose."*
— Dolly Parton

When I speak to groups about the importance of mourning well
as a precursor to living well again, I often say that our
goal is to "live on purpose."

What does it mean to live on purpose? It means to be aware of
our own hopes, dreams, and values, and to live each day
in alignment with and pursuit of them.

The "on purpose" part requires consciously stating and
repeatedly checking back in with our intentions. It might also
require listening for the whisper of our intuition and following a
plan of action we've created for ourselves.

What's the difference between on-purpose you and willy-nilly
you? Both of you might live in the now, but only one
of you lives in intentional seeking of meaning.

*I want to live my life on purpose.*

# JULY 31

*"Let us not look back in anger, nor forward in fear,
but around in awareness."*

— James Thurber

Emotions aren't good or bad. They just are. And befriending
them as they naturally arise in us is part of
our mindfulness practice.

Fear and anger are normal and necessary human emotions, but
mindfully engaging with them means getting to know them and
seeking to understand why they come up. When we train the
light of our awareness on them, we often find that they are ego-
based responses. They are also resistance to what is.

If we experience anger or fear today, let's stop, breathe, and try
to understand what the true, deepest sources of the anger and
fear are. Anger is usually fear underneath. And what is the fear
about? What are we afraid of, and why? Exploring our fears
helps us tame them and live more fully in the now.

*I will not look back in anger, or forward in fear,
but around in awareness.*

# AUGUST 1

*"Keep yourself bright and clean. You are the window through which you see the world."*

— George Bernard Shaw

Thinking of our consciousness as a window can be a helpful metaphor as we work each day to live mindfully.

A mind cluttered with random thoughts and worries is akin to a dirty window. When we clean the window, we are able to think clearly and free ourselves from worries about the past and future.

A curtained window is a mind entirely closed off from the now. It does not truly see, hear, smell, feel, or taste what is happening in the present. It may also have erected a barrier against the truth of challenging feelings. Removing the curtain allows the mind to engage with the fullness of life.

When we catch ourselves living mindlessly, let's remember to clean our windows and fling open the curtains.

*I will clean my window and fling open the curtains.*

# AUGUST 2

*"Motivation is what gets you started.*
*Habit is what keeps you going."*

— Jim Ryun

Mindfulness is a habit. Like all habits, the more we practice it,
the more ingrained and automatic it becomes.

Recent studies show that it takes about two months of
continuous practice for a habit to start "sticking."
If you work the meditations in this book most days,
you'll be reinforcing your mindfulness practice.

Incorporating a bodily routine into our mindfulness practice
will help ingrain it. For example, if I put my hands in my lap
and close my eyes for a few seconds each time I intentionally
move to recenter myself, this pair of actions becomes body
memory, and body memory moves us more readily into
the desired state. Choose a sequence of physical
actions and positions that feels right to you.

*Mindfulness is a habit. Intentional use of body memory can*
*help me reinforce my habit.*

# AUGUST 3

*"Why must conversions always come so late?*
*Why do people always apologize to corpses?"*
— David Brin

The now is pure potential. You have the power to make
powerful things happen. Right now.

In the next five minutes, you can right an old wrong. With one
simple phone call, email, or text, you can reach out to make
amends with someone you've long wanted to reconnect with
or apologize to. That's all it takes.

Living in the now does not mean suppressing or denying
regrets, not if they keep tugging at you, trying to get your
attention. Instead, it means engaging with them as they arise. It
means doing something about them in the now.

So visit, call, email, text, or write a letter.
Today is the day. This now is *the* now.

*Today I will reach out to right an old wrong.*
*This now is the now.*

# AUGUST 4

*"Life can be magnificent and overwhelming — that is the whole tragedy. Without beauty, love, or danger, it would almost be easy to live."*

— Albert Camus

You've probably learned by now that life is tragic. It's magnificent one moment and devastating the next. Its wild swings and randomness make it really, really hard to be human sometimes.

But beauty, love, and danger—the three very things that most readily break our hearts are the same three things that make life worth living. What would our lives be without beauty, love, and risk-taking? Dullsville, that's what. Meaningless. Empty.

Our challenge is to cultivate awareness of beauty (and its counterpart, ugliness), love (and its twin, grief, as well as its opposite, hate), and danger. To be present to them. To embrace them in the now. They are why we're here. Come what may, they are the best of what life has on offer.

*Beauty, love, and danger are both the tragedy and the triumph.*

# AUGUST 5

*"My expectations were reduced to zero when I was 21.*
*Everything since then has been a bonus."*

— Stephen Hawking

At the age of 21, theoretical physicist Stephen Hawking was just finishing up his schooling at Oxford when his speech became slurred and he grew increasingly clumsy. He was diagnosed with amyotrophic lateral sclerosis, also called ALS or Lou Gehrig's disease. Doctors gave the rising young star two years to live.

But more than 50 years later, Hawking is still alive. Though progressively paralyzed, wheelchair-bound, and unable to speak without the aid of a machine, he defied the odds and went on to make many noteworthy contributions in the field of cosmology. What's more, he was married twice and fathered three children, with whom he is reportedly still close.

How do you live with a life-threatening illness? In the now. How do you live knowing you could die any day (which is true of all of us, by the way)? In the now. Hawking has made the most of his uncertain nows. I hope we will too.

*My tomorrows are uncertain. Every day is a bonus.*

# AUGUST 6

*"There is something in every one of you that waits and listens
for the sound of the genuine in yourself. It is the only true
guide you will ever have. And if you cannot hear it,
you will all of your life spend your days on the
ends of strings that somebody else pulls."*

— Howard Thurman

Have you found yourself in your mindfulness practice yet? Have you trained yourself to hear the whispers of your soul and focus your awareness on the flicker of your unique divine spark?

Many people struggle with finding the one-of-a-kind genuine inside them. In a culture so obsessed with busyness and constant distraction, it's no wonder.

If you're having a hard time unearthing or connecting with your purposes and passions, I suggest spending some mindfulness time each day with that intention in mind. After all, until you feel right with your timeless self, you will never feel truly anchored and at home in the now. Mantras and meditation will often bring you closer. For some, conversation with close friends or a counselor helps them understand themselves better. Journal writing, yoga, and activity therapies (such as art therapy) can also help.

*Every day I seek and listen for the sound of the
genuine in myself.*

# AUGUST 7

*"It's not always that we need to do more but rather*
*that we need to focus on less."*

— Nathan W. Morris

Oh boy am I guilty of this one. I'm so hell-bent on helping others and wringing the most from every day that I take on too much. I'm a recovering Type A. I've managed to achieve an A- so far, but I'm working on a B+.

Less is more. This is a helpful mantra for people like me. When I catch myself saying "yes" to too many commitments at once, I mindfully remind myself: Less is more.

We don't need to constantly multitask to seize the day. What we need is to mindfully unitask. We need to focus fully on one important activity or person at a time, in the now. In between periods of concentrated focus, we need to rest.

Simplify. Simplify. Simplify.

*Fully focusing on one important activity or person at a time,*
*in the now, is my goal.*

# AUGUST 8

*"If you keep getting stuck in past memories, you can't fully focus on the present and create good memories for the future."*
— Donald Hill

As a grief counselor and educator, I know how important it is to explore memories at a time of loss. Memories are the best legacy we have after someone loved dies, and actively remembering helps us process our grief. I often say that it's essential to go backward before we can go forward.

But if you find yourself getting stuck in past memories, whether they're related to someone who has since died or to anything else (often one kind of loss or another), that's a sign that you probably need help getting unstuck. Seeing a compassionate talk therapist for at least a few sessions will likely help you move out of the past and into the present.

We must listen to the music of the past to sing in the present and dance into the future. That's another thing I often say. But if listening to the music of the past is consuming you, you won't be able to sing in the present or dance into the future. I hope you will schedule an appointment with a counselor. It's the most mindful, self-loving thing you can do.

*I must go backward before I can go forward.*

# AUGUST 9

*"An intention is a directed impulse of consciousness that contains*
*the seed form of that which you aim to create. Like real seeds,*
*intentions can't grow if you hold on to them. Only when you*
*release your intentions into the fertile depths of your*
*consciousness can they grow and flourish."*

— Deepak Chopra

Physician and spiritual guru Deepak Chopra believes in the
power of intention. He agrees that taking time to consider what
you would like to happen—in your life,
in your day—is time well spent.

But Chopra also asks us to have an attitude of hope and ease in
holding our intentions. He believes that intentions formed from
a place of contentment are much more powerful than intentions
created from a feeling of lack or need.

If we trust that all is well and we release our intentions after
touching lightly on them each day, we are more likely to see
them realized, says Chopra. We are also more
likely to enjoy the now.

*I touch on my intentions lightly each morning then*
*release them to my consciousness.*

# AUGUST 10

*"When you repeat a mistake, it is not a mistake anymore.
It is a decision."*

— Paulo Coelho

We all make mistakes. And if we're going to take risks and actively pursue our dreams, which I hope we all are, then we're going to make lots of mistakes. That's a good thing.

But if we find ourselves repeating the same mistake over and over again, that's not a good thing. It's probably a sign that we need to apply more awareness and discernment to the issue.

Why do we keep making the same mistake? What is the source of the unhealthy pattern? Being mindful about the thoughts and emotional process we go through that leads up to the mistake each time and talking it over with friends of good judgment will help us better understand our own blind spots. Mindfulness is a tool for self-understanding as well as self-direction.
Let's remember to use it both ways.

*If I'm making the same mistake over and over, that means I must apply more awareness and discernment to it.*

# AUGUST 11

*"I have come to believe over and over again that what is most
important to me must be spoken, made verbal and shared,
even at the risk of having it bruised or misunderstood."*

— Audre Lorde

Audre Lorde was a poet and civil rights activist in the 1900s.
Out of necessity, she came to understand one of the most
important precepts of mindfulness: speaking your mind is just
as important as knowing your mind.

What happens when we think and/or feel something very
powerfully inside of us but never—or rarely—express it?
Quite simply, we are living a lie. We are not declaring our truth.
We are withholding our ineffable essence.
We are watching the dance but not dancing.

Being aware and expressing are both
essential to living fully and congruently in the now.
One without the other is but a half-life.

*I am aware of my inner knowing, and I
express my inner knowing.*

# AUGUST 12

*"I understand now that the vulnerability I've always felt is the greatest strength a person can have. You can't experience life without feeling life. What I've learned is that being vulnerable to somebody you love is not a weakness, it's a strength."*

— Elisabeth Shue

More and more I have grown to realize that vulnerability may be the crux of this whole mindfulness endeavor.

When we are mindful, we train our awareness. But when we add vulnerability to the mix, we open our awareness to whatever may come. We don't avert our gaze from the scary or difficult things our awareness might notice. We also don't allow our fears to prevent us from being and expressing our most genuine selves.

We can't experience life without feeling life. We can't live mindfully in the now without truly feeling the now. We can't live fully in the now without acknowledging and embracing all of the now. Turns out vulnerability is the most underrated superpower.

*To truly live in the now, I must be fully vulnerable in the now.*

# AUGUST 13

*"To change one's life: Start immediately.*
*Do it flamboyantly. No exceptions."*

— William James

The best time to plant a tree was 20 years ago.
The second best time is now.

You've probably heard this Chinese proverb. It's popular because it does two things. It acknowledges that it is human nature to procrastinate, even on important actions. And it reminds us that as long as we're still alive, it's not too late.

Whatever you've long been meaning to do but haven't, you've been meaning to do it for a reason. It's stuck with you all this time because it's important to your soul.

You're not being mindful if you're routinely setting aside Big Things. What you're being is incongruent.
You're lying to yourself.

To really and truly live this day with mindfulness, you are called upon to finally act. Now. No exceptions.

*I'm not being mindful if I'm not doing what my*
*soul has long been asking me to do.*

# AUGUST 14

*"The goal of life is to make your heartbeat match the beat of the universe, to match your nature with Nature."*

— Joseph Campbell

Whenever I am fatigued or stressed, or I catch myself spinning in a mindless loop, I step outside. The natural world never fails to calm me and help me put things in perspective.

Sometimes I sit on my deck, appreciating its mountain views or, at night, the starlit skies. Sometimes I go for a hike. Sometimes I am fortunate to sink my toes into a sandy beach.

It's easy to be mindless amid the hustle and bustle of everyday life. It's much harder to be mindless when you are surrounded by nothing but God's creation. Mindfulness and presence are at home in nature. Let's remember that the next time we're struggling with our mindfulness practice.

*Mindfulness and presence are at home in nature.*
*I will remember this when I'm struggling*
*with my mindfulness practice.*

# AUGUST 15

*"Live to the point of tears."*

— Albert Camus

One good gauge of how often we are spending our time on the things that are truly meaningful to us is the frequency with which we are moved to tears.

Think about the times in your adult life that you have cried. Several that spring to mind for me are when my children were born, when my kids achieved certain milestones (like my firstborn Megan's recent wedding), the deaths of loved ones, encounters with nature, and the rare grief counseling session in which the person's loss circumstances were so tragic and traumatic that shared tears were the only human response.

What can I learn from this accounting? My children move me. My family and close friends move me. Nature moves me. My career moves me. The more time I spend in intimate interaction each day with these things, the more I will be living fully and on purpose.

What moves you to tears? Do that.

*I am moved to tears by* _____, _____,
*and* _____. *I will devote more time to them.*

# AUGUST 16

*"We are what we love."*
— Erik Erikson

The famous 20th-century psychoanalyst Erik Erikson, who coined the term "identity crisis," believed that during our middle years, from the age of 40 to 65, we naturally begin to understand our roles in the bigger picture. It is during this time, he believed, that we find an appreciation for the lasting meaning to be found in serving others.

If we are generating meaning—by activities such as raising children, helping others at work, or volunteering in our communities—we feel good about ourselves. If, on the other hand, we sense that our daily lives are devoid of meaning, we feel at loose ends or even despair.

Mindfulness helps us be intentional about pursuing activities that feel meaningful to us. When we mindfully choose how to spend our time, then live in the now of that chosen time, we are living our best life, on purpose.

---

*I intentionally choose to pursue activities that feel meaningful to me.*

# AUGUST 17

*"Don't bend; don't water it down; don't try to make it logical;*
*don't edit your own soul according to the fashion. Rather, follow*
*your most intense obsessions mercilessly."*

— Franz Kafka

One friend of mine loves to fish. He'll hike miles upon miles
just to cast his hand-tied fly into a remote mountain lake.
Another friend is a football guy. He knows all the stats by
heart—for all the teams—and manages his fantasy team with
the fervor of an NFL coach. A third friend makes handcrafted
ukuleles. He's always been a woodworker, but for some reason
ukuleles are his latest obsession, even though
he doesn't play the instrument himself.

Our passions aren't always logical. They don't always make
sense to others. But if they feed our souls, it doesn't matter.

What are your obsessions? Do you mindfully make time for
them? Today, follow at least one of them mercilessly.

*I follow my most intense obsessions mercilessly.*

# AUGUST 18

*"It is amazing what you can accomplish if you
do not care who gets the credit."*

— Harry S. Truman

Our souls often want to make contributions to the world. We
have instinctive impulses to help others and to right wrongs.

But wait a second, our egos say. If we're going to be heroes,
we should be recognized. Credit where credit is due
and all that jazz.

Mindfulness helps us be aware of and ignore the vanity of our
egos. Living in the now helps us act when we have the impulse
to act. Together the two forces create the conditions necessary
for us to get stuff done without regard to self-aggrandizement.

It's not about us. It's about what's right and good.

*It's not about me. It's about what's right and good.*

# AUGUST 19

*"I went to the woods because I wished to live deliberately, to front only the essential facts of life, and see if I could not learn what it had to teach, and not, when I came to die, discover that I had not lived. I wanted to live deep and suck out all the marrow of life."*

— Henry David Thoreau

What are the essential facts of your life?

Thoreau famously went to live alone in a primitive cabin in the woods to discover the answer to this question. But we don't have to remove ourselves entirely from our homes and our current lives to do so.

As we move through this day, we can ask in each moment: Is this essential? Is this essential? Is this grooming habit essential? Is this car (and the time and money I devote to it) essential? What about this internet habit? Is it essential?

Anything we encounter that does not give us a burst of connection, love, or meaning when we question it is inessential. It can go. This is how we mindfully winnow our lives down to their essence and suck all the marrow out of life.

*Anything I encounter in my day that does not give me a burst of connection, love, or meaning is inessential. It can go.*

# AUGUST 20

*"The job is not your work. What you do with your heart and soul is the work."*

— Seth Godin

I am fortunate to earn my living doing something I feel passionate about. Not everyone is so lucky, I realize.

If you are among the millions of people who work at a job that does not feed your soul, mindfulness and living in the now can still help you find meaning in your work hours. Strive to be aware of other people and your own attitude. Be present to the tasks at hand. Mindfully incorporate walks, healthy food, kindness, gratitude, and social interaction into your day. Remember that academic and career accomplishments don't matter nearly as much as the ways in which you helped other people and how you made them feel.

At the same time, consider your true work, which is what you do with your heart and soul. Of all the activities you put effort into, which really matter to you? How can you devote more time to those and less to others?

*My true work is what I do with my heart and soul.*

# AUGUST 21

*"Be the person your dog thinks you are."*

— J.W. Stephens

Have you ever come home at the end of a long, crappy day only to have your spirits lifted by a wagging dog or shin-rubbing cat? (I know others of you love horses, birds, goats, and all varieties of companion animals; I include them in this discussion, too!)

I know I have—many times. Our pets simply adore us. They're thrilled to see us. At my house, our dogs come ecstatically running to greet us every time we walk in the door and follow us around like they're groupies and we're rock stars.

What do our pets want from us? Food and shelter. A kind voice. A gentle touch. Sometimes adventures together in the great outdoors. Most of all, they just want us to be with them.

That's living in the now, in a nutshell.

*I am working to be the person my companion animal thinks I am.*

# AUGUST 22

*"Whenever sorrow comes, be kind to it. For God has placed a pearl in sorrow's hand."*

— Rumi

It takes courage and fortitude to befriend our sorrows.

"But it hurts too much!" we want to say. "I don't want to be sad! I don't want to grieve!"

And yet we must. Ignoring, suppressing, or denying pain is something our culture encourages, but encountering pain is the only path that leads to true healing and growth. Engaging with the sorrow we naturally experience in life is the mindful choice.

And when we are mindfully kind to sorrow, it one day rewards us with the pearl it holds in its hand.

*Engaging with the sorrow I naturally experience in life is the mindful choice.*

# AUGUST 23

*"Rituals are the formulas by which harmony is restored."*
— Terry Tempest Williams

Rituals are powerful shortcuts to meaning.

The biggest rituals of our lives—such as baptism, graduation, weddings, funerals—are rites of passage. Everyday words and actions aren't significant enough to mark those occasions, so we have used rituals since the beginning of time to help us move through them.

In our daily lives, our sacred little rituals provide similar bursts of meaning and structure. Meditating with our morning coffee or eating dinner together every night as a family demonstrates our commitment to what we know to be truly important.

If you seek to commit to something with more intention, mindfully ritualize it in some way. This helps elevate it from the hubbub of normal life, making it the sacred activity you believe it to be.

---

*Adding ritual to any activity elevates it. I can choose to ritualize anything I want to deepen my experience of.*

# AUGUST 24

*"None of us get out of life alive, so be gallant, be great, be gracious, and be grateful for the opportunities you have."*

— Jake Bailey

Diagnosed with Stage 4 lymphoma a week before graduation, New Zealand high school senior and class captain Jake Bailey was scheduled to give a speech at his graduation ceremony. Even though he'd begun receiving chemotherapy and wasn't feeling great, the courageous young man delivered the inspiring speech anyway. It quickly went viral and is still available for viewing on YouTube.

Sometimes young people are forced into maturity by circumstances. They're thrust into developing a perspective that many people who are much older don't yet have. When this happens, we are well served to listen to them.

"I don't know where it goes from here for any of us—for you, for anyone, and as sure as hell not for me," Bailey said at the end of his address. "But I wish you the very best in your journey, and thank you all for being part of mine."

As of this writing, Bailey is in remission and says that he tries to make the most of every day.

---

*Jake, I promise to try to be gallant, great, gracious, and grateful.*

# AUGUST 25

*"Done is better than perfect."*
— Sheryl Sandberg

Many people suffer from analysis paralysis. That's the tendency to think and think, plan and plan, but never do.

The thinking and feeling part is essential. Locating and befriending our inner knowing is always Step One. It's also Mindfulness 101.

But my God, we're made to interact in and with the world! We have senses that capture what is going on outside us. We have miraculous bodies that give us the capacity to do so much. We have speech! We have language to express what we are thinking and feeling.

Internal pondering and feeling. External action. If your living-in-the-now seesaw tips too much in either direction, it's time to rebalance.

*I ponder and I act. I feel and I do.*

# AUGUST 26

*"A disciplined mind leads to happiness, and an undisciplined mind leads to suffering."*

— Dalai Lama

Hey, wait a minute! Living in the now is all about doing whatever feels good in the moment, right? Hakuna matata. Don't worry; be happy!

It turns out that living in the now, when uncoupled from intention and discipline, is empty. It's devoid of meaning. And in fact, it often leads to suffering.

The disciplined mind reads books on mindfulness. It steps outside the now of incessant, random thoughts and impulses to consider values and goals. It directs the course of each day with intention.

Deeply considered discipline is mindful and essential to our wellbeing.

*I must live in the now, but with intention and discipline.*

# AUGUST 27

*"One of the secrets to staying young is to always do things you
don't know how to do, to keep learning."*

— Ruth Reichl

In her 50s, my wife decided to take lessons in Spanish and
Italian. She's a travel aficionado and runs a women's travel
group, and she wanted to be able to better communicate
when she visits other countries. (As a matter of fact,
I'm with her in Rome, Italy, right now!)

The now presents us with myriad opportunities. We have free
will, and many of us are fortunate to have hours of free time
each week. How should we spend them? Using some of them to
learn and grow is a way to engage more deeply in this amazing
opportunity called life. Besides, learning is associated with
better cognitive health and often better physical, emotional,
social, and spiritual health.

As we age, we're at risk for getting more and more stuck in
routine habits. Let's remember to shake it up. Intentionally,
mindfully incorporate some learning into your day.

*Today is a day for learning.*

# AUGUST 28

*"Toddlers know that there are far more important things to focus on than how our hair looks or how we're perceived by others."*

— Doug Motel

When we're really trying to inhabit the now, we'd be well-served to behave like toddlers.

How do toddlers act? They live thoroughly in the moment. They engage with whatever they find most captivating within their reach. They touch everything. They interact with everyone and every living thing. They explore. They authentically express every emotion. In their view, everything is good until proven otherwise.

What don't they care about? They couldn't care less about how you look or how much money you make or what kind of car you drive. They just want to interact with you and learn from you.

Immersion. Joy. Human interaction. Authenticity. No judgment. No ego. The toddler school of now comes highly recommended.

---

*For at least a few minutes every day, I will behave like a toddler.*

# AUGUST 29

*"Absence sharpens love. Presence strengthens it."*
— Thomas Fuller

If you want to build stronger relationships, mindfully create
more opportunities to spend time together.

There is no substitute for presence. It's as simple as that. Oh
sure, you can "keep in touch" with lots of people via texting
and social media, but you can't be a true part of someone's life if
you're not interacting regularly, face to face.

We often love people who live far away, but love and attachment
grow much stronger with the simple miracle of presence.

Who do you want to be present to today?
Find a way to make it happen.

*I find ways to be present to the people I care about.*

# AUGUST 30

*"The sun tires of summer and sighs itself into autumn."*
— Terri Guillemets

An Indiana native and a Coloradan for decades, I've always lived somewhere with four distinct seasons. I appreciate the unique beauty and opportunities of each season, and I'd miss them if I relocated to a climate with less variation throughout the year.

But regardless of where you live, summer's end brings changes. The transition to the new season affects our lives in myriad ways, from a shift in wardrobe and menus to growing darkness to a return to indoor activities and more cocooning.

As we mindfully move into autumn, let's consider the season ahead. How do we want to spend it? What do we hope to accomplish? What is most important to us in the next three months? Taking a few minutes at the start of each new season to plan and choose our intentions will help us live in the coming now with meaning and purpose.

*I note the change of seasons, and I make plans.*

# AUGUST 31

*"You know what's really, powerfully sexy? A sense of humor. A taste for adventure. A healthy glow. Hips to grab onto. Openness. Confidence. Humility. Appetite. Intuition. ... Smart-ass comebacks. Presence. A quick wit. Dirty jokes told by an innocent-looking lady. ... A storyteller. A genius. A doctor. A new mother. A woman who realizes how beautiful she is."*

— Courtney Martin

What do all these attributes have in common? Positive engagement with and in the now.

When you meet the now head-on with positive, genuine intentions, you are a force to be reckoned with. As Martin says, you might be confident or you might be humble, but either way, you're here. You're veritably buzzing with aliveness.

Don't hold back. Work on being your fullest self in the here and now.

*When I meet the now head-on with positive, genuine intentions, I am a force to be reckoned with.*

# SEPTEMBER 1

*"You cannot move things by not moving."*

— Suzy Kassem

This day and every day, we commit to ACT mindfully.

In psychology circles, the acronym ACT stands for Acceptance and Commitment Therapy, which is a rising star in the mindfulness movement. It combines mindfulness with action. It links awareness with behavior—a combination we've been talking about a lot in this book.

When you work with a counselor on ACT, you hone your ability to be present to your life while also moving toward your desired goals.

In this pragmatic philosophy, ACT is also a mnemonic reminding you to: Accept your reactions and be present to them; Choose a direction that aligns with your values; and Take action. Accept. Choose. Take action.

This and every day, we commit to ACT mindfully.

*I Accept, Choose, and Take action.*

# SEPTEMBER 2

*"This journey has always been about reaching your own other shore no matter what it is, and that dream continues."*

— Diana Nyad

Long-distance swimmer Diana Nyad was the first person confirmed to have swum from Cuba to Florida—110 miles— without a shark cage. She was 64 years old.

You're here. Your biggest, fattest, hairiest goal is over there. That's *your* other shore. How will you get from here to there?

With mindfulness and intention.

Of course, it doesn't really matter if you actually get from here to there…unless your goal continues to stir your soul. If your passion fades or you begin to feel more compelled by a different aim, by all means, change course. Then you'll have a new shore to reach.

*I can get to my other shore with mindfulness and intention.*

# SEPTEMBER 3

*"Cherish forever what makes you unique,*
*cuz you're really a yawn if it goes."*
— Bette Midler

Right now, make a list—on paper or in your mind—of the top
three ways in which you are unique.

Got it?

How many of these attributes are you proud of? Which do you
deploy to their maximum advantage? Which do you tend
to ignore or downplay, and why?

Like all of us, you sparkle in certain ways. The world needs your
idiosyncrasies. We need your unique contributions. How boring
the world would be if you weren't unapologetically you in all the
nows of this day—and all the nows of the days to come.

*Without my idiosyncrasies, my life would be boring.*

# SEPTEMBER 4

*"Art enables us to find ourselves and lose ourselves at the same time."*
— Thomas Merton

Making art can be a powerful way both to understand ourselves and to be present in the moment.

When we sketch, paint, take photos, assemble a collage, play music, write a poem or song, craft, make a mini-movie, or participate in any kind of artistic endeavor, we are living in the now as well as plumbing the depths of our subconscious.

Immersing ourselves in art that others have created also provides us with this two-pronged opportunity.

Whether we make or appreciate art, we may at once lose ourselves in the experience and find ourselves in the experience. Let's work some art into our day.

*Art can help me both lose and find myself.*

# SEPTEMBER 5

*"A lot of the conflict you have in your life exists simply because you're not living in alignment; you're not being true to yourself."*
— Steve Maraboli

As we work on living more mindfully, let's pay special attention to two things: our anger and our fear.

Anger and fear indicate conflict. When we feel upset or afraid, it's because we perceive a reality or possibility in the world that conflicts with what we want or know to be true. There's a mismatch between what's inside of us and what's outside of us.

And sometimes the conflict arises purely inside of us, such as when we want two seemingly different things.

Mindfulness can help us get to the bottom of these conflicts. Often what we need is to spend more time in meditation and quiet contemplation to understand how to be true to ourselves. When that happens, conflict begins to resolve and we feel the peace and wellbeing of congruency.

*Anger and fear indicate I'm not living in alignment with myself.*

# SEPTEMBER 6

*"Follow effective actions with quiet reflection. From the quiet reflection will come even more effective action."*

— Peter Drucker

Peter Drucker was the influential business thinker and author who predicted many of the most significant workforce trends of the last 100 years. Throughout his 95 years, he was a busy guy. He was an economist, professor, and founder of one of the first MBA programs. He wrote 39 books and countless articles for the likes of *Harvard Business Review, The Atlantic,* and *The Economist.*

What's more, Drucker was a good guy. He championed people over profits and believed that only noble companies are great.

Drucker understood how to be effective, and he taught organizations how to be effective. He pointed out that the most effective business people came with a wide variety of personality attributes, but all shared a focus on how they spent their time and which efforts produced the most desirable results.

Essentially, Drucker lived mindfully and extolled mindfulness. He believed that the now is a tool to wield with intention and compassion. As the quote above captures, he also thought that effective action must be interspersed with periods of quiet contemplation. We would all be well served to learn from Drucker.

*I act effectively then reflect. Then I act effectively again.*

# SEPTEMBER 7

*"It's astounding how much one's stress level goes down with the simple act of switching from skinny jeans to yoga pants."*

— Author Unknown

Physical wellbeing is a prerequisite to complete presence. When we're feeling unwell, in pain, weak, hungry or thirsty, overly tired, or uncomfortable, our bodies are asking for our attention. Until we give them that attention, they will keep pulling our awareness in their direction.

So let's be mindful of what makes our bodies feel good— and what doesn't. Exercise, healthful food, ample water, excellent healthcare, and adequate sleep are essential. Comfortable clothing, too.

Jammies and slippers, anyone?

*My physical wellbeing is a prerequisite to presence.*

# SEPTEMBER 8

*"I choose to make the rest of my life the best of my life."*
— Louise Hay

Perhaps the best thing about getting older is that with each passing day, we learn. We make decisions and blunder ahead, and eventually we realize that we understand more now than we used to. We know better what to do and what not to do. We appreciate what matters and grow more relaxed about letting go of everything else.

Life is full of ups and downs, but because we're learning all the time, we're trending upward. Actually, studies show that people's self-reported wellbeing falls a bit from young adulthood to about age 50 then climbs and climbs after that, eventually reaching a higher level than it did in youth.

Mindfulness and intention can help us ensure that the rest of our lives will be the best of our lives. Let's choose to make it so.

*With mindfulness and intention, I will choose to make the rest of my life the best of my life.*

# SEPTEMBER 9

*"When you discover that all happiness is inside of you, the wanting and needing are over, and life gets very exciting."*

— Byron Katie

Byron Katie was 43 when she had a depressive breakdown. After checking herself into a halfway house, she encountered an insight that changed her life. "I discovered that when I believed my thoughts, I suffered, but when I didn't believe them, I didn't suffer. And this is true for every human being."

Katie went on to develop a method of self-inquiry she calls "The Work." It consists of four questions she calls turn-arounds. When you're stuck on a belief that's making you unhappy, she says, you must ask yourself four questions: 1. Is is true? 2. Can you absolutely know it's true? 3. How do you react, what happens, when you believe that thought? 4. Who would you be without the thought?

Mindfulness helps us examine and choose our thoughts. Often we have the power to pick more constructive and equally (or more) valid thoughts than the ones that were making us miserable. This is our Work today.

*I can choose to relinquish thoughts that are making me miserable and replace them with thoughts that motivate me.*

# SEPTEMBER 10

*"You can't imagine just how much believing in negative thoughts
is affecting your life…until you stop."*
— Charles F. Glassman

Many of us are our own worst enemies. We self-sabotage by
allowing our fears to flourish, making mindless choices, and
spinning in endless loops of wishing-but-not-doing.

But mindfulness is the essential tool to help us break the self-
sabotage cycle. First we notice our harmful thought patterns.
We study and name them. We might write them down or talk
about them with a good listener. We embrace them with self-
compassion. Then we choose more effective thought patterns.
And we mindfully work on integrating them into our daily lives,
until they, too, become habits.

If we are stuck in self-sabotage thinking, our attempts to live in
the now may only reinforce our destructive thought patterns.
Mindfulness can lift us up and out.

*Mindfulness can lift me up and out of self-sabotage thinking.*

# SEPTEMBER 11

*"You can't be that kid standing at the top of the waterslide, overthinking it. You have to go down the chute."*

— Tina Fey

There's a fine line between mindfulness and overthinking, right?

If we jump willy-nilly on every opportunity that comes our way today, we'll be whirling dervishes! That's not effective. But if we stop and agonize over every choice, we'll spend too much time frozen in inaction. We'll be stuck. That's not effective either.

Meditation and intention help us choose our paths in advance. We identify heartfelt goals and commit to taking steps that lead us toward them. If one of our goals is to be more open to adventure, for example, we can more readily say yes to adventurous opportunities that arise spontaneously in our day. We don't need to stand at the top of the waterslide, overthinking it, because we've decided in advance that we're going to go down the chute.

Overthinking is a self-defeating habit for many people. Let's work to replace it with true mindfulness.

*I will replace overthinking with mindful action.*

# SEPTEMBER 12

*"Dying seems less sad than having lived too little."*
— Gloria Steinem

As a grief counselor and educator, I understand that the death of
someone we love causes normal and natural sadness.
Dying is an irreversible loss that is just plain sad.

But it's not the saddest thing. Not even close. The saddest thing
is dying while you are alive. It's putting up walls around your
heart so that you're not vulnerable. It's not loving enough. It's
not risking enough. It's spending too much of your precious
time and energy on things that don't really matter.

When we are mindful of this distinction, we live in the now
with intention and purpose. We have gratitude for each day.
We live fully.

We will die. The people we love will die. These are
unalterable truths. But not all of us will really live.
I hope you are one who will.

*Not everyone really lives. I intend to.*

# SEPTEMBER 13

*"The only way around is through."*
— Robert Frost

Since I am fortunate to live in Colorado's Rocky Mountains, I hike a lot. I enjoy decompressing by spending time in nature, away from civilization and technology.

When I'm on a trail and encounter a downed tree or a creek that's breached its banks, I go around. I swing wide and head off trail in order to bypass the obstruction. It's safer and faster than plunging headlong into the problem area.

But life's biggest challenges don't work that way. When we try to go around them, we end up making things worse. If we're having relationship troubles, ignoring them is a recipe for disaster. If we're in a financial bind, pretending everything's OK will only get us further in the hole. If someone we love dies, trying to go around our grief instead of through it turns us into the living dead.

The more we practice stepping bravely into the now of our challenges, the more we will be rewarded with grace, hope, and reconciliation.

---

*The more I step bravely into the now of my challenges, the more I will be rewarded with grace, hope, and reconciliation.*

# SEPTEMBER 14

*"Be in love with your life. Every minute of it."*
— Jack Kerouac

Because my work involves speaking in cities across the country and around the world, I regularly experience all the indignities and annoyances of travel. Interminable security lines. Delayed and canceled flights. Inconsiderate seatmates. Lost luggage. Dangerous taxi rides. You name it; I've had it happen.

But because it allows me to share my passion with the world, I try to love travel. I try to marvel at all the good things it brings into my life. I've spent time in hundreds of cities. I've met thousands of amazing people. I've had dozens of randomly transformative experiences.

On especially fatiguing days, I'm not successful at loving my itinerant lifestyle. But I find that when I'm able to marshal mindfulness, it helps me be present to the good without overreacting to the not-so-good.

*I am in love with my life. Almost every minute of it.*

# SEPTEMBER 15

*"Hold the hand of the child that lives in your soul.*
*For this child, nothing is impossible."*

— Paulo Coelho

When you were a kid, what did you want to be when you grew
up? What were you passionate about? What made you gleeful?
What did you dream about? What did you wish for?
What did you love?

I agree with Coelho: That child is still inside you. Cultivating an
awareness of your inner child can often help you live with more
meaning and purpose in your present.

Today, talk with two or three people who knew you when you
were a child. Ask them to describe what you were like and what
you cared about. In their memories you just might find clues
that can help bring your life full circle.

*I am reacquainting myself with the child who lives in my soul.*

# SEPTEMBER 16

*"A funny thing happens when we start keeping promises to ourselves. We become unstoppable."*

— Ken Fite

Human behavior researchers used to think that willpower was a limited resource. When people became fatigued by delaying gratification in one way, they were more likely to go off the wagon in another. Or so the studies seemed to demonstrate.

But this theory of ego depletion recently has been cast into doubt. It's now thought that we don't run out of willpower— but we may run out of passion. We simply don't care about certain things as much as we care about others.

So let's make promises to ourselves about the things that matter most to us, and let's cut ourselves some slack on self-disciplinary to-dos that are essentially trivial. Let's not sweat the small stuff, but let's mindfully and tenaciously sweat the big stuff.

Gotta go. I've got promises to myself to keep.

---

*To me, some things are important and some are not.*
*I will keep promises to myself about the important stuff.*

# SEPTEMBER 17

*"We do not need magic to change the world. We carry all the power we need inside ourselves already. We have the power to imagine better."*

— J.K. Rowling

Somewhere along the way, you were probably told that you could accomplish anything you set your mind to. Want it. Envision it. Then go make it happen.

Our imagination may be our most powerful capacity. It's what has led to humankind's most marvelous inventions, discoveries, and accomplishments. Someone wanted them, envisioned them, then went and made them happen.

In our own small lives, our imagination helps us visualize possible realities that stir our souls. Imagination is a magical mindfulness tool. Time spent imagining is spirit time. It helps us reach for better.

Now lift your imaginary wand, and imagine what it could create.

*I have the power to imagine better.*
*I also have the power to make it happen.*

# SEPTEMBER 18

*"I've found that sitting in a place where you have never
sat before can be inspiring."*
— Dodie Smith

We've all heard the adage "Bloom where you're planted." It's
a good one. Living in the now requires acceptance of what is.
When we fully embrace this moment, we are blooming
where we are planted.

But when we find ourselves in a new place or unfamiliar
circumstances, or when we mindfully and intentionally position
ourselves in a different place or situation, we're encountering an
opportunity for growth. How will we respond to the new?
How will we live fully in the now of the new?

Change is often challenging, and when it tears us away from
things and people we are attached to, it necessitates a period of
mourning and reconciliation. But change is also exciting. If we
mindfully engage with its opportunities, we are living
fully and on purpose.

What newness can we bring into our lives today?

---

*New places, people, and situations can rouse me and
help me live fully and on purpose.*

# SEPTEMBER 19

*"I think my biggest achievement is that after going through a rather difficult time, I consider myself comparatively sane. I'm proud of that."*

— Jacqueline Kennedy Onassis

None of us gets through life unscathed by loss and grief. Some of us suffer more traumatic or trying circumstances than others, but we all suffer.

When we come out on the other side of a painful situation, we feel like survivors. Things may not be perfect, but we made it. Whew. We're still here. We're still alive and kicking.

At these moments, it's appropriate to celebrate our survival. Despite its many imperfections, life is good. Let's live in the now of our gratitude. Let's use what we've learned to fuel our passion for this day and all the precious days to come.

*I celebrate my survival. I live in the now of my gratitude.*

# SEPTEMBER 20

*"When you kill time, remember that it has no resurrection."*
— A.W. Tozer

Are you using your precious time on the things that matter most to you?

In one study, a group of women were asked which voluntary activities they derived the most satisfaction from. They put prayer, worship, and meditation at the top of their lists and watching TV near the bottom, yet they spent much more time each day watching TV than they did on their spiritual activities.

Right now, make a list of the things (people, activities, passions, pursuits, goals) that you love most. Now make an effort to spend every free minute you have today on items on this list. Save five minutes for the end of the day so you can write about the ways in which this day was different than most.

*I apportion my time according to my priorities.*
*This is mindful living in the now.*

# SEPTEMBER 21

*"I imagine one of the reasons people cling to their hates so stubbornly is because they sense, once hate is gone, they will be forced to deal with pain."*

— James Baldwin

Anger and hate are normal human emotions—but they aren't fundamental emotions. Instead, they are shoots that explode from the roots of fear.

Which feels better—anger or fear? Anger arises from ego. It feels active and just. Fear, on the other hand, makes us feel vulnerable. We fear loss, which causes us pain. We choose anger because it's an anesthetic.

In this way, both anger and hate are not mindful emotions. Rather, they are a mask we have learned to place over our vulnerability and fear. Our mindfulness practice requires us to befriend our anger and hate in order to better understand what they are masking. Where do we feel vulnerable? What are we afraid of?

Learning to live mindfully in the now of our anger and hate means caring for them as we would care for toddlers. They require lots of attention, gentleness, understanding, and self-compassion. Letting them run amuck, on the other hand, is bad parenting.

*My mindfulness practice requires me to befriend my anger, hate, and fear to understand what they are trying to teach me.*

# SEPTEMBER 22

*"The body heals with play. The mind heals with laughter.*
*The spirit heals with joy."*

— Proverb

This advice is so great you might want to write it down on a sticky note or commit it to memory. In any given moment, it can help you resurface from mindless thoughts or behaviors and find opportunities for richness in the now.

Let's play today. What kinds of play do you enjoy? Sports, board games, puzzles, craft-making, engaging with children—anything you find playful counts.

Let's laugh today. What tickles your funny bone? Comedy shows or movies, friends who make you laugh, engaging with children—anything you find funny counts.

Let's seek joy today. What gives you joy? Hiking to a mountaintop, stargazing, holding your beloved's hand, baking bread—anything that sparks joy for you counts.

*My body heals with play. My mind heals with laughter.*
*My spirit heals with joy.*

# SEPTEMBER 23

*"It is inner stillness that will save and transform the world."*
— Eckhart Tolle

I need this reminder today. On days when I find myself worked up over seemingly insurmountable hurdles—in my personal or family life, in my career, in the world at large—I would be well served to take some time to still myself and turn inward.

When I stop to close my eyes and focus on my breath, I reduce my awareness to this moment. In this moment, I am here. I am well. I am in touch with my eternal soul.

If everyone on earth were to practice mindful stillness each day, imagine what a different world we would live in. Tensions fall away. Gratitude and compassion expand. Beauty and love rise.

I am working on being in the world with that inner stillness strong inside me.

*For me and for you and for all of us, it is inner stillness that will save and transform the world.*

# SEPTEMBER 24

*"Life is more fun if you play games."*
— Roald Dahl

If you've ever played a fast-paced game of Monopoly or a
rousing match of croquet, you know that games
require our attention.

We're present when we play games, whether they're board
games, card games, or sports like ping-pong or baseball. (My
personal favorite is basketball with my son, Chris.) What
happens when we play games? We relax. We socialize. We
converse. We laugh. We lose ourselves in the moment.

Old-fashioned games are an antidote to multitasking and
electronics. They're a healthy, more mindful alternative to
watching TV or frittering away time online. Invite a family
member or friend to play a game with you tonight in lieu
of your usual routine. See what happens.

*When I make time to play games, my life is more fun.*

# SEPTEMBER 25

*"If you don't pay appropriate attention to what has your attention, it will take more of your attention than it deserves."*

— David Allen

Multitasking is counterproductive. In fact, recent studies show it reduces our productivity by a whopping 40 percent.

What's more, multitasking increases the production of stress hormones. When we're trying to do multiple things at once, we're triggering a cortisol cascade and feeding a dopamine addiction. Our prefrontal cortexes—the parts of our brain that control decision-making and help us focus—like novelty, so they're excited by multiple, varied inputs. (Texting, internet surfing, and watching TV all at the same time, anyone?) But while the multitasking dopamine is making us feel good in the moment, we're not being mindful or effective.

Working on paying attention to one thing at a time is mindfulness in action. When we pay appropriate attention only to what really needs or deserves our attention, we're living in the now with effectiveness and presence.

*Only when I am paying attention to the one thing that really needs and deserves my attention am I living in the now with effectiveness and presence.*

# SEPTEMBER 26

*"No matter how difficult and painful it may be, nothing sounds as good to the soul as the truth."*

— Martha Beck

What does the truth have to do with living in the now?

When we are inhabiting a lie, we cannot be genuinely present. Part of us is always standing over there, with the truth. It's as if our consciousness becomes split. We may try to ignore or deny the true part, but we can't—not really. It keeps trying to get our attention, tugging on our shirtsleeves in odd moments and waking us up at night.

Inhabiting the fullness of the now requires mindfully embracing the truth. Even when the truth is hard and we would rather pretend not to see it, it is an essential prerequisite to presence.

Are there any truths we've been avoiding? Today we will turn toward instead of away from them.

*Mindfulness requires me to turn toward and honor the truth.*

# SEPTEMBER 27

*"There are people who have money and people who are rich."*
— Coco Chanel

For something that supposedly makes the world go 'round, money is a remarkably flimsy commodity. Above a certain modest point—after basic needs are met and a feeling of stability achieved—wealth doesn't make people happier. Study after study has confirmed this.

Imagine you could have ten million dollars deposited in your bank account today, no strings attached, OR you could be given a guarantee that the none of the people you love would come to any sort of harm for at least the next ten years. Which would you choose? In an instant it becomes clear what true wealth is.

When we are mindful about money, we learn to separate our feelings of fear of lack and its flip side, striving for more, from what is really essential in our lives. We become aware of how to truly enrich our precious days. We make choices that make us richer in the ways that count.

*I want to be rich in the ways that count.*

# SEPTEMBER 28

*"Everyone shines, given the right lighting."*
— Susan Cain

Picture a cut diamond. If you place it in the light and slowly turn it, it sparkles. That's because individual facets catch and reflect the light. As you continue to move the diamond, facets that were sparkling go dark and new facets catch fire.

That's how people are. In the right circumstances, every individual will sparkle. Their unique gifts and passions will be shown to greatest effect, and they will shine with remarkable brilliance. Living in the now requires non-judgment. We must accept people as they are, even when they've gone dark.

In what circumstances do you shine? Mindfully cultivating your awareness of this will help you choose to shine more often— and be self-accepting when it is your turn to recede into the shadows.

*I accept myself and others, both when we are sparkling and when we go dark.*

# SEPTEMBER 29

*"I love when conversations and energies just flow. Not forced.
Not coerced. Just present."*

— Dau Voire

Here's a living-in-the-now trick: Stop and chat
with more people.

Strike up a conversation in the grocery store or at the post
office. Talk to your neighbor instead of simply waving hello.
Learn more about your coworkers and service providers.

What you'll find is that small talk isn't small. It's the very stuff
of presence and of life. It connects you to others and develops
empathy. And sometimes long-lasting, meaningful relationships
arise—relationships that could imbue your life with even more
richness, purpose, and grace.

I challenge you to start a conversation with at least one random
person today. After, notice how your feelings for that person
have changed or deepened.

*Acknowledging and talking to others is always a
worthwhile activity.*

# SEPTEMBER 30

*"Only when your consciousness is totally focused on the moment you are in can you receive whatever gift, lesson, or delight that moment has to offer."*

— Barbara De Angelis

Whenever we allow ourselves to be absent in the moment, we are missing out. Thinking mindless thoughts and doing mindless things take our consciousnesses away from the present. We're here, but we're not really here. And whatever's unfolding right in front of us? It's whizzing past us, unnoticed.

Mindless living is a lot like sleepwalking. We're seemingly up and moving, but we're not really aware of what's happening. We might as well climb back into bed.

Today, as we repeatedly return our straying thoughts and behaviors to the now, let's notice all the little gifts, lessons, and delights we encounter. The more aware we become, the more tiny miracles we experience.

*Only when my consciousness is totally focused on the moment I am in can I receive whatever gift, lesson, or delight that moment has to offer.*

# OCTOBER 1

*"Love is the strongest force the world possesses, and yet it is the humblest imaginable."*

— Mahatma Gandhi

I defy you to name anything more powerful than love.

Yes, hate is powerful too, and it causes suffering, but even in the face of suffering, love triumphs. It saves and soothes us. It gives every day meaning. When we are surrounded by hate and fear, we cling to love. When we are surrounded by love, we surrender to it.

Love is strong yet humble. Can something really be both? Can we be both? Absolutely. Mindfulness and living in the now keep our egos in check and foster beneficial vulnerability, but they also allow us to stand strong, with arms wide open, come what may.

*Love is strong yet humble. I am strong yet humble.*

# OCTOBER 2

*"The authentic self is soul made visible."*

— Sarah Ban Breathnach

Do you ever try something new and think, "Interesting.
But it's not 'me.'"?

That voice you hear is your authentic self. It lets you know what
feels "right" and what feels "wrong." We also call it "instinct"
or "gut feeling."

When your inner knowing matches your outward behavior, you
feel at home in your life. Things click. Mindful awareness helps
you pay attention to this sense of congruency (or lack thereof)
between the inner and the outer.

It's important to try new things, though. Often our hesitation
before we even try something isn't inner knowing—
it's fear and self-doubt. Give it a go before you allow your
authentic self to weigh in.

---

*When my inner knowing matches my outward behavior,
I feel at home in my life. I feel congruent.*

# OCTOBER 3

*"Follow your interests, get the best available education and training, set your sights high, be persistent, be flexible, keep your options open, accept help when offered, and be prepared to help others."*

— Mildred Spiewak Dresselhaus

That pretty much covers it.

Sprinkle in plenty of being present in and embracing the moment, and you've got everything you need.

By the way, Millie Dresselhaus, born in 1930, was a professor emerita of physics and electrical engineering at MIT. She's known for her scientific contributions to carbon nanotubes and low-dimensional thermoelectrics. Her research made possible many of our current electronics, including smartphones. In 1990 she was awarded the National Medal of Science and later the Presidential Medal of Freedom.

Whatever your interests are, I hope you'll go after them in the manner of Millie.

*I will go after my interests in the manner of Millie.*

# OCTOBER 4

*"Remember then that there is only one important time,
and that time is now. The most important one is always the one
you are with. And the most important thing is to do
good for the one who is standing at your side."*

— Jon J. Muth

Today, love the one you're with.

Be present to the people around you. If you're having breakfast
with your partner, be fully aware of and communicate intensely
with your partner. If you're meeting with a colleague, pay close
attention to your colleague. If you're spending time with
your children, give them your whole self.

Being present to and serving the people we love is the most
mindful, nowful, meaningful way to spend our time.
Let's remember that then.

*Being present to and serving the people around me is the most
mindful, nowful, meaningful way to spend my time.*

# OCTOBER 5

*"Without a sense of urgency, desire loses its value."*
— Jim Rohn

During the course of your life, what are some things you deeply desired but never pursued? Perhaps relationships, hobbies, education, travel, careers, financial goals, and more come to mind.

Now, of those things, for which is it too late?

Life moves swiftly. Opportunities pass us by. Unless we match our desires with a sense of urgency, it's all too easy for years and then decades to slip away. And before we know it, it's too late.

But we live and we learn. That's how life works. And if we've learned this poignant lesson, that means we'd damned well better apply it to what we desire now. Today, we will urgently, urgently, urgently pursue something we care about but haven't yet committed to or completed.

*Today I will urgently pursue something I care about but haven't yet committed to or completed.*

# OCTOBER 6

*"I am not so enamored of my own opinions that I disregard what others may think of them."*

— Nicolaus Copernicus

Copernicus was the astronomer who revealed that the Earth rotates around the sun and not, as was believed before that, the other way around.

And yet even Copernicus, who revolutionized astronomy, was interested in hearing what other scientists had to say. He held the truth in higher esteem than his own theories.

Our egos like to think they're right. Our mindfulness practice helps us kennel our egos so that we can take in other kinds of understanding, including the opinions (and research) of others. Like Copernicus, we pursue the truth. But we also pursue connection and kindness. These are yet higher values.

Let us not be so enamored of our own opinions that we disregard what others think and, just as important, feel.

*I am not so enamored of my own opinions that I disregard what others think and feel.*

# OCTOBER 7

*"Self-care is never a selfish act—it is simply good stewardship of the only gift I have, the gift I was put on earth to offer to others."*

— Parker Palmer

Self-neglect is mindless. Good self-care is mindful.

When we are mindful of our own physical, cognitive, emotional, social, and spiritual needs, we are aware of how our choices each day affect our wellbeing. We simply feel better when we are taking good care of ourselves, and mindfulness makes this clear.

Our lives are gifts—both to ourselves and to others. What do you do with the most precious gift you've ever been given? You take care of it so that you and others can enjoy it as fully and as long as possible.

*My life is a gift. I take excellent care of it so that I and others can enjoy it as fully and as long as possible.*

# OCTOBER 8

*"Bring Presence into whatever you do."*
— Eckhart Tolle

I like this quote because we're used to focusing on being present as we live in the now. Here we're being asked something slightly different, which is to bring our Presence into whatever it is we are doing.

As we drive to work, we can remember to bring our Presence into our bodies behind the wheel. As we chop onions for dinner, we can remember to pick up the knife with Presence. As we fold the laundry, we can remember to inhabit the activity with our Presence.

Tolle says that the moment we realize we are not being present, our Presence appears. And the more we practice bringing our Presence into everything we do, the more automatic it becomes.

Right now, bring Presence into the activity of holding and reading this book. It's like your soul and body and mind snap together. All three parts are attuned and aligned.
Presence is present.

*I will bring Presence into everything I do.*

# OCTOBER 9

*"Would that there were an award for people who come to understand*
*the concept of enough. Good enough. Successful enough.*
*Thin enough. Rich enough. Socially responsible enough.*
*When you have self-respect, you have enough."*

— Gail Sheehy

"Enough" is a wonderful mindfulness concept—one we can call
on as a mantra in every moment of annoyance, dissatisfaction,
and even boredom.

If I'm stuck in traffic and I feel my blood pressure building, I
can remind myself that there is enough time to do what really
needs to be done that day. When I've invited friends over and
am fretting in the moments before their arrival about the stain
on the carpet or my old couch, I can remind myself
that my home is enough.

In this moment, I am enough. In this moment, you are enough.
As long as we have shelter and food and people who
care about us, we have enough.

Enough with mindless worries. Enough is enough.

*In this moment, I am enough, as are you.*

# OCTOBER 10

*"Mindfulness gives you time. Time gives you choices. Choices, skillfully made, lead to freedom. You don't have to be swept away by your feeling. You can respond with wisdom and kindness rather than habit and reactivity."*

— Bhante Henepola Gunaratana

Time is our most precious resource. Our efforts to live in the now and stay mindful are proof of this. Both acknowledge that time is a gift that should never be squandered or lived mindlessly.

When we are aware of how we are spending our time, we learn that we have choices. We can rise above the chatter of our constant thoughts. We can acknowledge how we are feeling yet choose to respond to our feelings with intention and kindness. We can decide what to do (and what not to do) in this moment and the next moment and the next moment ad infinitum.

Mindfulness frees us to live how we want to live and be who we want to be in every amazing moment. What a revelation.

*Mindfulness gives me the time and awareness to be who I want to be.*

# OCTOBER 11

*"It's a helluva start, being able to recognize what makes you happy."*
— Lucille Ball

Have you gotten to the point in your life where you increasingly recognize that things that are supposed to make you happy don't always make you happy?

Take big vacations, for example. Do they make you happy, or do they stress you out? Or fancy cars. They're fun to drive, but they're expensive to own. Is it worth the tradeoff to you? And what about something as simple as that TV show you binge watch? Does it really make you happy, or has it merely become a mindless routine?

With mindful awareness, we can figure out what gives us joy. The more mindful we become, the more we may be surprised when we weigh our options. Society pushes certain values on us, and our upbringing also imposed a value system, but mindfulness helps us nudge those powerful influences aside so that we can listen to that still, small voice inside of us.

*I am working on recognizing what truly makes me happy and gives my life meaning.*

# OCTOBER 12

*"Meditation is not a way of making your mind quiet. It is a way of entering into the quiet that is already there, buried under the 50,000 thoughts the average person thinks every day."*

— Deepak Chopra

Some of us (me included) think we've failed at meditation when we find that we're unable to stop our minds from thinking random thought after random thought. But meditation masters don't eliminate thoughts. Instead, they acknowledge them as they rush by but choose not to engage with them.

Picture yourself sitting inside a rock cave behind a waterfall. You are safe and dry and comfortable. You are meditating. Your thoughts are like the water rushing past you. You cannot stop them. Your goal is not to stop them. Your goal is simply to allow them to flow by and not concern yourself with them. Your thoughts have their own agenda. You don't have to try to answer their questions or solve their problems. You are safe and dry and comfortable.

As with any exercise, we get better at finding and inhabiting the quiet cave inside us the more we practice. It's a worthwhile endeavor. It can change your life.

*Each day I will practice finding and inhabiting the quiet cave inside me.*

# OCTOBER 13

*"In dwelling, be close to the land. In meditation, go deep in the heart."*

— Lao Tzu

Living in the world and inner contemplation—we mindfully toggle back and forth between these two practices.

We can think of them as the yin and yang of our days. In Chinese philosophy, the yin-yang symbol depicts the complementary nature of opposite forces. They are inextricable; they cannot exist without each other.

Yin is the dark or shady side. It is night. It is quiet. It is rest, contraction, and descent. To me, meditation is yin. Yang is light and energy. It is activity, expansion, and rising. To me, living in the now is yang.

Within each half of the yin-yang symbol is a drop of the other. In meditation, we are also living in the now. In living in the now, we can also maintain a meditative consciousness. The two forces are inextricable; they cannot exist without each other.

*I am yin, and I am yang.*

# OCTOBER 14

*"Whatever you're meant to do, do it now. The conditions are always impossible."*

— Doris Lessing

I'd really like to_____, but there's this hurdle and this hurdle and this hurdle...

Sound familiar? Not only is it in our nature to find excuses, but there are often legitimate reasons why we can't do what we'd like to do. There's not enough time, education, money, support. We're too fat, broke, busy, old.

But here's the thing: The conditions are always impossible. Bill Gates' first business was a bust. Stephen King's first novel manuscript (for *Carrie*) was rejected thirty times. And Steven Spielberg couldn't get into film school at the University of Southern California because his grades were too low. They rejected him twice. You can bet that in all of these cases, other circumstances were less than ideal as well.

Just begin. Your notion that a better time will arise is only a myth borne of fear.

*The time is never perfect. I must begin anyway.*

# OCTOBER 15

*"Patience and perseverance have a magical effect before which difficulties disappear and obstacles vanish."*

— John Quincy Adams

I'll be the first to admit that I'm not naturally the most patient person. I'm more than a little ADD, to be honest. It's hard for me to concentrate on one task for a long period of time. I'm better at focusing for short bursts then moving on to the next activity. When something is taking too long, I get impatient.

But as I've gotten older and more mindful, I've grown more patient. I'm still ADD, but I'm aware of it now. When I feel antsy, I allow myself to get up, move around, and change focuses, but I also know that I will return to my earlier task later in the day. If I feel my short fuse burning up as I communicate with others, I take a breath and insert some mindful distance into the conversation.

Good things come to those who wait and who persevere. Mindfulness is patient and intentional. Together these are magical qualities.

*I am mindfully patient. I mindfully persevere.*

# OCTOBER 16

*"Flow is the natural, effortless unfolding of our life in a way that moves us toward wholeness and harmony."*

— Charlene Belitz and Meg Lundstrom

When life feels easy and pleasurable, and the universe seems to present us with just what we need when we need it, we're experiencing the energy called "flow." Synchronicities arise. We float the path of least resistance. We're aware and joyful.

In my experience, life doesn't always flow. Obstacles and losses naturally cross our paths. But when we feel especially stuck or stymied, it's a good idea to try going with the flow.

If you white-water raft the Colorado river near my house, the guides will teach you that if you end up in the water, you should float face-up, with the current, your feet down-river. The water is too powerful to swim in, so you have to float. Keeping your feet in front of you prevents your head from striking a rock. Lying flat will allow you to breathe easily as you skim over obstacles.

If you're dumped into the rapids of life, lie back and float for a while. Relinquish control and stay safe. Trust that trusting in life's synchronicities will carry you to dry land.

*When I'm tossed into the rapids of life, I give myself permission to lie back and float for a while.*

# OCTOBER 17

*"How much of your life do you spend looking forward to being somewhere else?"*

— Matthew Flickstein

This is one of the most maddening challenges of our age. Electronic media, especially, has made it so easy and so tempting to be everywhere but where we are.

With a swipe of our finger, we can be on a different continent (or galaxy), in a different era, with different people, among different ideas and different sensory experiences. Of course, as electronics grow more sophisticated, technologies like virtual reality and holograms will only make non-locality and non-presence more possible and alluring.

Then there is the good old-fashioned type of yearning for what is to come, such as looking forward to when our kids are grown or putting all our hopes on our next vacation.

Planning, hoping, imagining, and dreaming can be wonderfully productive (and I would say, essential) ways to spend some of our time, but they are not living in the here and now. For that we need to be where we are now. Most of us allow too much time to slip by on the former, robbing us of the latter. Let's work on finding a better balance.

---

*I will devote more time to living in the here and now.*

# OCTOBER 18

*"The world is full of magic things, patiently waiting for our senses to grow sharper."*
— William Butler Yeats

People with one sensory deficit often develop heightened abilities in their other senses. Blind people, for example, may have superior hearing skills. We used to think that was because blind people paid more attention to what they heard and leaned on that input more heavily than sighted people, but now we know that they are using their brains differently.

Thanks to the brain's ability to change and adapt with experience, an attribute called neuroplasticity, it can literally rewire itself. One study showed that people who are born deaf use areas of the brain normally devoted to sound for processing touch and vision instead.

Mindfulness can have a similar effect. The more we train our senses through awareness, the more our brains adapt to process the additional input. Essentially, we develop super sensory powers, which in turn reveal a world of magic.

*Awareness reveals a world of magic.*

# OCTOBER 19

*"A schedule defends from chaos and whim. It is a net for catching days. It is a scaffolding on which a worker can stand and labor with both hands at sections of time."*

— Annie Dillard

Can you live in the now *and* carefully adhere to a day calendar on your phone or on paper?

Yes. Think of schedules as scaffolding for goals and dreams. Some of the things we schedule are mundane tasks that support bigger goals. A dentist appointment, for example, may not be an important goal unto itself, but maintaining our health is absolutely essential if we are to live well and long, and accomplish our heart's desires.

Then there's breaking down gigantic goals into small, daily steps. Figuring out and adding the small steps to our day-to-day schedules keeps us mindful of completing them.

Of course, we can go overboard. Overscheduling our days will keep us from enjoying the now and is a form of mindlessness itself. Yet eschewing schedules altogether will likely keep us pinballing from one random activity to another—another form of mindlessness. A happy mix of scheduled and unscheduled time is the sweetest spot.

---

*I aim for a happy mix of scheduled and unscheduled time.*

# OCTOBER 20

*"The desire to reach for the stars is ambitious.*
*The desire to reach hearts is wise."*

— Maya Angelou

I certainly hope you have passions and goals, and that each day
you're leveraging your mindfulness to chip away, bit by bit, at
fulfilling them. Yes, I believe you have unique gifts
that this world needs.

Reaching for the stars is both exciting and admirable. But along
the way, it's also essential to be mindful of the *whys* behind your
ambitions. If you desire wealth and status, for example, you will
not find fulfillment in those realms unless you also desire to use
your wealth and status to help others. See how that works?

Wisdom is mindfulness that keeps the *whys* front and center.
If you can be ambitious in ways that reach hearts (including
yours!), your wisdom can transform the world.

*I am ambitious in ways that touch the hearts of others*
*as well as my own heart.*

# OCTOBER 21

*"If your goal is to avoid pain and escape suffering, I would not advise you to seek higher levels of consciousness or spiritual evolution."*
— M. Scott Peck

Yikes.

As we unroll ourselves from the bubblewrap of mindlessness, we begin to encounter the world and our consciousness in more authentic ways. Under the bright-white light of awareness, beliefs, behaviors, relationships, and values that we once held dearly often start to crack and crumble.

It can be a sort of loss, awakening to the truth. It hurts. We often have to break away from old habits, people, and ways of thinking. We have to take time to mourn what we're leaving behind before we can fully step into our newly heightened consciousness.

But it's worth it. Mindfully living in the now infuses our lives with a richness and depth that was impossible before. It's like going from watching an old cathode-ray-tube TV to the highest-def flat screen you can imagine. And once you make the switch, there's no unseeing the clarity now possible.

*Awakening can be painful, but it is worth it.*

# OCTOBER 22

*"Instinct is the nose of the mind."*

— Madame de Girardin

As a child of children of the Depression, I'm a believer in not letting things go to waste. Plus, I recently learned that food waste is one of the top five contributors to climate change. Combine those two things and you can imagine how I feel about throwing away perfectly good food.

Here's my rule: If you pull something out of the refrigerator and it looks OK—no mold, no slime, no odd color—then give it the sniff test. If it smells OK too, it's probably fine to eat.

Our instincts are the sniff test of our minds. If our instincts are telling us something is off, it probably is. If, on the other hand, our instincts give us the green light, then we can probably safely proceed.

Not sure how to mindfully decide about something? Give it the sniff test.

*I will trust my instincts. They are the sniff test of my mind.*

# OCTOBER 23

*"Inaction, contrary to its reputation for being a refuge,
is neither safe nor comfortable."*
— Madeleine Kunin

The dying understand this all too well.

On their deathbeds, many people express regrets that they
spent too much of their lives *not* doing: not expressing their true
feelings, not pursuing their true goals, not spending enough
time with those they loved most.

In other words, they regret inaction. Inaction seemed safe
and comfortable at the time, but with the benefit of life's final
hindsight, they realize that inaction turned out to be unsafe
and uncomfortable. It was a trickster and a fraud.

Action in the now will be our mindful intention for this day.

*Ultimately, inaction is neither safe nor comfortable.
I will act on my highest desires today.*

# OCTOBER 24

*"Listening is much more than allowing another to talk while waiting for a chance to respond. Listening is paying full attention to others and welcoming them into our very beings. The beauty of listening is that those who are listened to start feeling accepted, start taking their words more seriously and discovering their true selves.*

*Listening is a form of spiritual hospitality by which you invite strangers to be friends, to get to know their inner selves more fully, and even to dare to be silent with you."*

— Henri J.M. Nouwen

Active listening involves training our full awareness on another human being. We set aside all distractions, and we draw close to the other person. We look them in the eyes. We regard them with empathy and kindness.

Whenever we are actively listening to a friend or family member, we are living mindfully in the now. This form of mindfulness not only helps ground us, it also provides the person who is speaking with spiritual hospitality. We are creating conditions for their divine sparks to shine forth and be recognized.

Learning to be better listeners is part of our mindfulness practice. Let's work on that today.

*Today I will mindfully listen.*

# OCTOBER 25

*"Work is either fun or drudgery. It depends on your attitude.*
*I like fun."*

— Colleen C. Barrett

I've been fortunate to have a career I'm passionate about.
In fact, I think of it as a calling, not a job. Not everyone ends
up earning a living with their calling. I understand that
it's not always possible, nor are callings always
activities that pay money.

But still and all, thinking of work as fun or drudgery is a choice.
I know a woman in her late 60s who works for my local city
grounds crew. She mows parks. She plants flowers. She digs
weeds. In the summer, her step counter regularly logs more
than 100,000 steps—over 40 miles—each week. It's a physically
strenuous job, but one she keeps because she needs the
money and the benefits.

Also, if you ask her, she'll tell you she loves her job. She loves
being outdoors, in God's creation. She revels in
staying strong and fit.

Her attitude about her work is a choice. Ours is too. I don't
know about you, but I like fun.

*I choose to enjoy my work. I like fun.*

# OCTOBER 26

*"You are the product of your own brainstorm."*
— Rosemary Konner Steinbaum

Here's to the power of brainstorming.

Spending time considering our passions, plans, and futures is time well spent. When we still ourselves to connect with our divine sparks and figure out how to align our days with what's most essential to us, we are brainstorming our lives.

Some brainstorming happens intentionally, perhaps through journaling or discussing life plans with a good friend or mentor. Some happens more mysteriously, through mindfulness practices such as meditation. And some happens subconsciously, when we are busy doing other things or daydreaming.

Spend at least a few minutes brainstorming your life today. It's a habit worth cultivating.

*I can brainstorm my own life.*

# OCTOBER 27

*"I will not let anyone walk through my mind with their dirty feet."*
— Mahatma Gandhi

Sometimes we may be vulnerable to external messages
of fear, anger, and hate.

When we are fatigued, we are vulnerable. When we have
suffered a loss of any kind, we are vulnerable. When we have
too much on our plates and are overly stressed,
we are vulnerable.

As we've discussed, vulnerability is a good thing because it
opens us to the full richness and truth of life. But we should be
mindful during stressful periods of vulnerability because if we're
not careful, they can spin us off into fear, anger, and hate.

Meditation, prayer, and other spiritual practices can help us
stay centered and hopeful, and resist the allure of mindlessness.
When we are aware of dirty feet, we can take care not to
let them into our house.

*Especially when I am already stressed, I will not let anyone
walk through my mind with their dirty feet.*

# OCTOBER 28

*"This is the art of courage: to see things as they are and still believe that the victory lies not with those who avoid the bad, but those who taste, in living awareness, every drop of the good."*

— Victoria Lincoln

Yes, it takes courage to live in the now. It's often hard to accept and embrace everything that is happening. Some of it is maddening. Some of it is painful. And yet that is our task and our quest: to be here now.

It's tempting to jump on the bandwagon of avoiding the bad. After all, if we just ignore everything that's painful, we can be happy all the time! Alas, that approach doesn't work. It only leads to a deadened, zombie-like existence.

We can, however, remain present to the challenging and the painful while also mindfully choosing to taste every drop of the good. If we live in the now of our pain, our reward is not only understanding and healing, it is the capacity to fully appreciate what is fine and pleasurable. Presence to heartbreak enables and enhances presence to joy.

*I will remain present to the challenging and painful while also mindfully choosing to taste every drop of the good.*

# OCTOBER 29

*"I think midlife is when the universe gently places her hands upon your shoulders, pulls you close, and whispers in your ear: I'm not screwing around. It's time. All of this pretending and performing— these coping mechanisms that you've developed to protect yourself from feeling inadequate and getting hurt—has to go. Your armor is preventing you from growing into your gifts."*

— Dr. Brené Brown

My psychology training and counseling work helps me quickly identify people's armor. Yet most aren't even aware of the protective mechanisms they use to shield themselves from vulnerability and pain.

Here are a few common armors I see: over-intellectualism (thinking instead of feeling); sarcasm; over-caretaking; addictive behaviors (not only alcohol and drugs but also gambling, shopping, sex, overwork, and more); and emotional detachment.

Anything that stands between you and your truest, richest, most present experience of life and other people is armor. It has to go. A few sessions with a good counselor may be enough to help you find ways to take it off.

---

*Each day I will mindfully take off another piece of armor.*

# OCTOBER 30

*"Anxiety's like a rocking chair. It gives you something to do,
but it doesn't get you very far."*

— Jodi Picoult

In the United States, it's thought that about 30 percent of adults aged 18 to 54 struggle with anxiety. If you're one of them, your mindfulness practice can help you be aware of your anxiety patterns and change your thinking and behavior.

Anxiety is mindless. Yes, people have legitimate and genuine worries, but spending a lot of time replaying those worries over and over in their minds causes mental and physical stress.

When you catch yourself in the rocking chair of anxiety—back and forth with the same worries, back and forth, back and forth—it's time to implement mindfulness practices. Try these: Meditate with a mantra, focus on and count your in and out breaths, listen to alpha-wave music, get up and take a walk, talk to someone who's a good listener.

Training yourself to become aware of and replace your anxious thinking and behaviors with more mindful ones can improve your quality of life many times over. If you need help making the shift, see a health coach or counselor. You'll be so glad you did.

*I am training myself to recognize my anxious thinking and
behaviors and replace them with more mindful ones.*

# OCTOBER 31

*"Courage is not the absence of fear but rather the judgment that something else is more important than fear."*

— Ambrose Redmoon

Mindful people are still afraid—they're just much less likely to let a burst of fear control their thoughts or dictate their actions. They see fear for what it is—a normal and even necessary human emotion that is almost always less important than mindful intention and enjoyment of life.

"I'm afraid to go to yoga class," our fear might tell us. "I'll look like a fool. I won't be able to do it."

"Pshaw," our mindful intention can reply. "I think yoga can help us in lots of ways, so we're going to give it a try."

Who was right? Mindful intention.

Your fear might save you from trying to beat a train across an intersection or gambling too much money away—hurrah for fear! But most of the time, it's to be hugged and acknowledged, like a child afraid of the dark, then tucked back in, kissed on the head, and left to soothe itself. It doesn't have the wisdom to be in control. There are other things that are much more important.

*Courage helps me see that my fears are not important.*

# NOVEMBER 1

*"Pared down to its barest essence, wabi-sabi is the Japanese art of finding beauty in imperfection and profundity in nature, of accepting the natural cycle of growth, decay, and death. It is simple, slow, and uncluttered—and it reveres authenticity above all."*

— Tadao Ando

The Japanese Zen Buddhist philosophy called *wabi-sabi* cherishes the wisdom and beauty of imperfection and brokenness. Our favorite chipped mug, a worn sweater our grandmother knitted for us, the lines on our aging faces— all of these are *wabi-sabi*.

In honor of this belief, some craftspeople practice an ancient art called *kintsugi,* which means "golden joinery." Kintsugi artists take broken pottery and china and join the fragments together with an epoxy that contains gold. The technique draws attention to and celebrates the imperfections.

Wabi-sabi is a shorthand for living in the now. When we see, feel, or experience something broken or imperfect, we are reminded to marvel at the natural imperfection—which is almost always, as it turns out, more interesting and perfect than perfect is.

*Imperfection is beautiful and desirable.*

# NOVEMBER 2

*"The pleasure which we most rarely experience*
*gives us greatest delight."*
— Epictetus

Old Epictetus, a Greek philosopher who lived in the first century A.D., gives us modern-day Americans, who live in an abundance he likely never could have imagined, a pretty good argument for mindful self-deprivation.

So much of what we desire is at our fingertips today. At a reasonable cost, we can instantly have all the food, drink, and entertainment we want. The trouble with this, of course, is that there's such a thing as too much of a good thing.

If we grab our favorite Starbucks drink twice a day, it's a daily routine. But if we only allow ourselves to have one a week, it's a treat we're likely to savor.

Which pleasures in our lives could use selective cutting back so that we will enjoy them more in the now?
Time for a little mindful pruning.

*Cutting back on certain pleasures sometimes makes them more*
*pleasurable and enhances the quality of my life.*

# NOVEMBER 3

*"We are all in need of mercy."*
— Dieter F. Uchtdorf

Mercy is mindfulness plus compassion. It may be the most transformative recipe in our handy-dandy mindfulness notebook.

Our egos judge. They tend to be coldhearted, black-and-white, even vindictive. Our souls, on the other hand, when we allow them to come forward, glow with mercy. They are our truest selves.

Mercy is the quality that empathizes with the many problems and frailties we all have. Mercy forgives. Mercy shows compassion. Mercy understands that to be human is to be beautifully imperfect.

When we tell our egos to sit down and be quiet, and invite our souls to stand up and speak, we are mindfully creating an opportunity for mercy to appear. Showing mercy to ourselves is an essential first step. Showing mercy to others is grace in action.

---

*Mercy is mindfulness plus compassion. I invite the quality of mercy into my mindfulness practice.*

# NOVEMBER 4

*"Everyone steps on the cosmic banana peel sooner or later."*
— Anne Lamott

To a large degree, life is an equal opportunity destroyer. Yes, I absolutely agree that some of us go through childhood and enter adulthood with more privilege than others, but none of us is safe from the whims of tragedy.

If you or someone you love has ever gotten life-alteringly sick or injured, lost a home or financial security, made a gigantic mistake that you can't take back, or suffered a significant loss or setback of any kind, you know that sometimes life punches you so hard in the gut that you can't breathe— for a painfully long time.

Mindfulness companions us through our seasons of despair. It helps us hold an intention to work toward healing. It reminds us to be hopeful. It brings our awareness back and back and back again to the present moment, where so many things are still miraculously good.

In those moments when we've slipped and are crashing hard, thank goodness for the cushion of mindfulness.

*Mindfulness will companion me through my seasons of despair.*

# NOVEMBER 5

*"The only joy in the world is to begin."*

— Cesare Paves

Hey, all you procrastinators out there…get going!

Having desires and dreams but not acting on them is like squirreling away a million dollars but never spending any of it.

After all, your desires and dreams are your soul's purpose here on earth. They're all your soul cares about, actually.

I hope you're already fulfilling some of your soul's desires through your relationships with others, your hobbies, and your work. But the ones you've let lay fallow— for God's sake, mindfully get yourself into gear.

To begin is to unleash a pent-up part of your spirit into the world. What a joyful freeing.

*It's time to get myself into gear.*

# NOVEMBER 6

*"Urgency means paying the details the attention they deserve, with the respect they deserve, without delay."*

— Richie Norton

I'm a car guy. I've learned the hard way that when a dashboard light starts blinking or a part starts wobbling, it's a good idea to take care of it right away.

One young man I know (who shall remain nameless) ignored the oil light on the late-model used truck his father bought for him. A few months later, the engine seized up, and the beautiful blue truck was, alas, totaled.

Some details in life really are unimportant, like whether your sandwich bun is toasted or not (though I prefer toasted). But other little stuff, like whether you had fried or grilled chicken on that sandwich, adds up quickly to big stuff.

Mindfulness helps us sort trivial details from essential ones. And living in the now with essential details means treating them with the respect and urgency they deserve. If we remain calm yet intentionally proactive, life is easier and more enjoyable. We reach our goals and fulfill our dreams. And we get to keep driving that beautiful blue truck.

*I am urgently mindful about the details that matter.*

# NOVEMBER 7

*"Life is to be enjoyed, not simply endured. Pleasure and goodness and joy support the pursuit of survival."*

— Willard Gaylin

Many times in this book we've talked about the importance of balancing enjoying the moment with the meaningfulness of pursuing longer-term goals. It's a worthwhile but challenging seesaw sometimes.

But now and then it's important to let loose. To heck with long-term goals and practical blah-blah. Let's just have fun!

Vacations are such a time. Adding in a few mini-vacations throughout each month is another joyful tactic. Smaller pleasures like a few hours at a spa, a stolen afternoon with your main squeeze, or a Netflix binge (complete with your favorite snack food) are pleasures that are pure fun but also support all the other hours and days of survival.

Take a pleasure break. You deserve it.

*Some hours and days are purely for pleasure.*

# NOVEMBER 8

*"In order to love who you are, you cannot hate the experiences that shaped you."*

— Andrea Dykstra

It's natural to feel shame and anger over things we did or things that happened to us in our lives, and as a grief counselor, I know it's necessary for us to explore and express our grief about these experiences.

But in working toward healing these old griefs, we are making peace with our pasts. We are reconciling ourselves to what happened and accepting that we are who we are because of it.

That doesn't mean we won't always feel twinges of anger, sadness, or regret, but it does mean that we mindfully acknowledge and embrace the wholeness of our selves—the good, the bad, and the ugly. Moving forward, we can then mindfully choose whatever steppingstones we want to get us from our current selves to the selves we want to become. All those coming steps we will take will in turn also become inextricable parts of us.

When we love ourselves fully, we love our entire selves.

*I accept and love all of me.*

# NOVEMBER 9

*"The universe is always speaking to us…sending us little messages, causing coincidences and serendipities, reminding us to stop, to look around, to believe in something else, something more."*

— Nancy Thayer

Boy, we sure notice a lot more when we start paying attention. These age spots on the backs of my hands, for instance. But I digress…

When we pay better attention in the now, things pop out at us in surprising ways. We start to pick up on patterns. We're more likely to notice coincidences.

Could it be that the universe is sending us little messages? Is it possible that the patterns aren't random coincidences but instead meaningful or guiding serendipities?

I don't know about you, but I'm game. I'm open to the possible mysteries of something else, something more. If mindfulness helps me not only live well today but connect with the divine, all the better.

---

*Mindfulness helps me live well today as well as believe in something more.*

# NOVEMBER 10

*"The only way to make sense out of change is to plunge into it, move with it, and join the dance."*

— Alan Watts

Change is movement, right? It's the shifting of this to that. It's the ending of one thing and the starting of another. Whether we asked for it or not, whether we like it or not, it's pushing us all the time.

We often resist. We try to plant our feet and stand firm. But change gives us a shove, and off we go.

Since we're moving anyway, we might as well go with the flow. Resistance only makes it harder, after all. If we plunge in and mindfully move with the change instead of against it, we're aligning with its transformative energies.

Might as well join the dance.

*When change comes along, I will dance with it.*

# NOVEMBER 11

*"To do the useful thing, to say the courageous thing, to contemplate the beautiful thing: that's enough for one man's life."*
— T.S. Eliot

This quote reminds me that I can never do/be/have it all.

No matter how mindfully I plan my days and how thoroughly I relish the now, I'm going to miss out on so many fantastic experiences during my brief earthly sojourn.

Fear Of Missing Out—or FOMO, as it's called—affects many of us. Ironically, whenever I'm caught up in FOMO, I'm Missing Out on fully being present to what's right here in front of me.

Usefulness. Courage. Beauty. Yes. Mindfully lived day in and day out, these three things are enough.

*Usefulness, courage, and beauty are enough for me.*

# NOVEMBER 12

*"If you could only sense how important you are to the lives of those you meet, how important you can be to the people you may never even dream of. There is something of yourself that you leave at every meeting with another person."*

— Fred Rogers

In his day, Mr. Rogers spent his career reminding all of us about how absolutely essential friends and neighbors are to one another.

How we choose to interact with and be present to others in the now creates ripples that carry on long after the interaction is over. The people we spend time with take the energy from our interaction with them and emanate that energy into their activities and their interactions with yet more people. It's a viral pattern that quickly spreads to hundreds then thousands then millions of others.

As we remember to be present and kind to other people today, we can carry Mr. Rogers' wisdom with us. We are important to those whose lives we touch, even in small ways. We are more important than we dream of.

*I am important in the lives of countless others.*

# NOVEMBER 13

*"The soul should always stand ajar, ready to welcome
the ecstatic experience."*

— Emily Dickinson

In my decades as a grief counselor, I've met quite a few people
who arrived at my Center for Loss with souls closed to the
experience we call life. They'd been hurt deeply by the death
of a loved one, and their hurt was often compounded by
unmourned losses earlier in their lives. To protect themselves
from their own pain as well as from the possibility of future
pain, they'd boarded up their hearts.

The good news is that they'd come to me because they knew
something was wrong. They usually didn't realize it, but they'd
come to me for help reopening the door.

When our hearts are open, we present our vulnerable, genuine
selves. We welcome the full breadth of experiences and
emotions. We are living in the now with no protective barriers.
We invite in the ecstasy—and agony—of life.

*My soul stands ajar, ready to welcome whatever may come.*

# NOVEMBER 14

*"If you have the capacity to be more than one thing,*
*do everything that's inside of you."*
— Bishop T.D. Jakes

What do you want to do? Who do you want to be?
The beauty of it is that you can pick many things, no matter
how chronologically advanced you already are.
As George Eliot famously said, "It's never too late to be
what you might have been."

Job-wise, the Millennial generation embraces the soul-attentive
imperative to do and be many things. In fact, they undertake an
average of four different jobs by the time they're 32—twice the
number of the generation before them.

But I'm not talking only about career here. I'm talking about the
full range of human endeavors, from relationships and travel to
hobbies and volunteering and everything else you can think of.

Be and do everything that's inside of you. Turn yourself
thoroughly inside out, then give yourself a good shake, to make
sure there's nothing still stuck in there that wants to come out.

*I want to be and do everything that's inside of me.*

# NOVEMBER 15

*"Abracadabra is actually an Aramaic phrase meaning*
*'I create as I speak.'"*
— Author Unknown

You are what you say, both silently to yourself and out loud
to others and the world.

Your words are magic that way. They create your reality. That's
how powerful thoughts distilled into language can be.

When we are mindful of our self-talk and our speech, we
choose words carefully. We select phrases that are kind,
compassionate, and positive. In situations in which we must be
critical, we take care to be constructively critical. We speak with
good intention and impeccable words.

The next time we're tempted to say something mean or snarky,
let's remember *abracadabra*. What is about to come out of our
mouths (or into our minds) has the power of magic.
As Glinda in *The Wizard of Oz* asked,
"Are you a good witch, or a bad witch?"

*I create as I speak. I will speak with kindness, compassion,*
*and good intention.*

# NOVEMBER 16

*"The purpose that you wish to find in life, like a cure you seek, is not going to fall from the sky… I believe purpose is something for which one is responsible; it's not just divinely assigned."*

— Michael J. Fox

I was only 14 when I realized what my calling was, but I know that many people struggle with figuring out their vocation.

"I don't love my job," people often tell me, "but I don't know what else I'd do…" Others say, "My life is going OK, but it seems like something is missing…" If you can relate, maybe it's time to set out on a mission to actively seek your purpose.

The noted women's health advocate Dr. Christiane Northrup says that our purposes can often be found in the things we were passionate about when we were children. In reconnecting with them as adults, we often find joy and meaning.

The author of the famous career guide *What Color is Your Parachute?*, Richard N. Bolles, says that your mission in life includes using your natural gifts that most delight you, in the places that most delight you, to help make the world a better place.

If your purpose doesn't fall from the sky, you're going to have to mindfully go find it. Good thing you're getting good at this mindfulness thing.

*I am mindfully seeking my purpose.*

# NOVEMBER 17

*"One way to open your eyes to unnoticed beauty is to ask yourself,
'What if I had never seen this before? What if I knew
I would never see it again?'"*

— Rachel Carson

These two questions have the power to snap us back to
presence when our monkey minds won't stop chattering.

*What if I had never seen this before?* In other words, what might I
notice first? What would strike me as interesting or odd? What
would I wonder about?

*What if I knew I would never see it again?* In other words, what
would I miss most? What should I commit to memory?

Unnoticed beauty awaits us everywhere we choose to focus our
awareness. Right now, notice a few of those things or beings.
Say a silent word of thanks.

*Unnoticed beauty is all around me,
waiting for me to become aware of it.*

# NOVEMBER 18

*"Life always bursts the boundaries of formulas."*

— Antoine de Saint-Exupéry

That's why living's so danged hard. Even if we mindfully, intentionally plan and execute, half the time things go awry. Life is just plain unpredictable. Unwanted change crashes down in front of us, like an old cottonwood in a windstorm. If we're not completely crushed, we can count ourselves lucky.

"The only thing you can count on is change," the saying goes. Don't we know it.

Living in the now is its own kind of formula, though. And it's a reliable one. Staying mindfully present to each moment gives us something to do when we don't know what to do.
It's a lifeline in the middle of a tornado.

Our lives will go off the rails now and then, guaranteed. When that happens, we can focus on hanging on to the here and now, which is as solid as solid gets.

*Staying mindfully present to each moment gives me something to do when I don't know what else to do.*

# NOVEMBER 19

*"The really important kind of freedom involves attention, and awareness, and discipline, and effort, and being able truly to care about other people and to sacrifice for them, over and over, in myriad petty little unsexy ways, every day."*

— David Foster Wallace

When we think about having the freedom to live in the now, we tend to imagine days filled with indulgent pleasures. You know, sleeping in, picking grapes off the vine, lying in a hammock, eating great food, watching the sun set. No work. No bills. No petty annoyances of any kind.

But when we apply mindfulness to this equation, we understand that the really important kind of freedom is not so lazy and hedonistic. Instead, it involves daily doses of intention, discipline, and effort.

Mindful freedom makes choices in pursuit of goals and dreams. It also spends a lot of time in service of others. It's often more drudgery than sexy, but it gives us a sense of purpose and meaning. That's what makes it really important.

*The really important kind of freedom involves mindful hard work and service to others.*

# NOVEMBER 20

*"Stay close to anything that makes you feel alive."*

— Hafiz

As father to three young adults, I see how slow and painful it can be to figure out what your true interests and passions are. Especially in this era of constant distraction and entertainment, it can seem like everything is interesting but nothing is compelling.

If you find yourself struggling with this issue now and then, ask yourself this question: What makes me feel alive?

Your answers don't have to have anything to do with a job or career, by the way. They just have to be something that makes you excited or glad to be here. Tiny little things and big things both count—and every size in between.

Got your list? Good. Now, mindfully build as many of these things into each day as you can without "ruining" them. Moderation will allow you to savor.

*How do I tell if something's a true interest or passion?*
*If it makes me feel alive.*

# NOVEMBER 21

*"Courage, dear heart."*

— C.S. Lewis

This three-word mantra is a good one to keep in
your back pocket.

So often mindful presence requires courage. Mindlessness is
easy; if something makes you uncomfortable or upset, you just
distract yourself from it with a mind-numbing activity.
Boom. Problem solved.

But mindfulness has a "no looking away" rule. We're committed
to being present to whatever's going on, as it's going on.
That takes courage.

But the "dear heart" part of the C.S. Lewis quote reminds
us to be self-compassionate too. We can be both brave and
empathetic at the same time. If we encounter something that
brings us to tears, it's natural and necessary to cry, for example.

So let's be both intrepid and tender. It's a winning combination.

*I will be courageous and self-compassionate both.*

# NOVEMBER 22

*"True happiness is an acceptance of life as it is given to us, with its diminishment, mystery, uncontrollability, and all."*
— Michael Gilbert

Life as it is given to us is a mixed bag.

Practically every day we suffer diminishments of one kind or another. Parking tickets, illnesses, unexpected bills. My house burned down a few years back. To add insult to injury, I'm getting shorter.

But when I remember to live in the now, it doesn't matter that I'm shorter. All that matters is this steaming mug of coffee, the pups at my feet, and the glory outside my writing hut's window.

If I embrace it all, the good and the bad, I live in a state of wonder. I can't control life, but by God I can marvel at the mystery.

*When I embrace the full gamut of experiences,*
*I live in a state of wonder.*

# NOVEMBER 23

*"Mastery requires focused repetition until it becomes an automatic program in your subconscious mind. Then your body knows better than your conscious mind."*

— Dr. Joe Dispenza

How do you get good at anything? You practice.

Malcolm Gladwell is the author and futurist who made famous the 10,000-hour rule. Essentially, the principle is that it takes 10,000 hours of practice at something to achieve mastery. To become a master pianist, accumulate 10,000 hours at the keyboard. To become a master golfer, spend 10,000 hours on the links.

Part of what happens with mastery is that your body starts to take over some of the work, freeing up your conscious mind for awareness of more nuanced performance.

The more we practice mindfulness, the more we master it. Also, the more our bodies take over some of the work. We breathe slowly and calmly without conscious instruction. We pause before reacting. We automatically reach for kindness and connection. How do you accumulate 10,000 mindfulness practice hours? One mindful day at a time.

*I am working toward banking at least 10,000 mindful hours.*

# NOVEMBER 24

*"The Buddha taught that anyone who experiences the delight of being truly generous will never want to eat another meal without sharing it."*
— Martha Beck

I hope you have personally experienced how love can transform life. I also hope you're mindfully working to appreciate love in the now and strengthen loving relationships.

Generosity is love's first cousin. It is the giving of yourself and your assets for the benefit of others. Like love and kindness, it immeasurably enhances our experience of living in the now.

True generosity requires giving without thought to receiving in return. Neither does true generosity worry that the giver may suffer a consequent lack. Instead, it trusts that there is plenty for sharing.

Be mindfully generous today. You may never want to stop.

*Whenever and wherever possible, I am mindfully generous.*

# NOVEMBER 25

*"And that is how change happens. One gesture. One person.*
*One moment at a time."*

— Libba Bray

You and I are always changing. We can't help it.
Change is the only constant of life.

Each day we get older. Each day we experience new
circumstances, thoughts, and feelings. Each day everything and
everyone around us changes a bit. Even during times when
daily changes are subtle, eventually we look back and
realize how different our lives are now.

All of this can and does happen without our awareness. But
when we add awareness and mindfulness to our days, we have
the thrilling opportunity to create change. No, we can't control
everything, and chaotic change will continue to swirl around
us. But we can shape important elements of our nows and our
futures if we set about directing certain changes with intention.

Today: One intentional gesture toward a change we desire.
One intentional moment at a time.

*I can direct change with intention.*

# NOVEMBER 26

*"For me, every hour is grace. And I feel gratitude in my heart each time I can meet someone and look at his or her smile."*

— Elie Wiesel

Holocaust survivor and Nobel Peace Laureate Elie Wiesel wrote about his concentration camp experiences in his famous memoir, *Night*. He was 15 when he and his family were sent to Auschwitz. His parents and a sister were killed. Along with two sisters, he lived to tell the tale.

Wiesel saw and experienced firsthand the horrors of man's inhumanity to man, yet he went on to write, speak, and teach about lessons learned and a better future. He emphasized bearing witness to one's own experiences—living in the now with them—while maintaining hope and faith.

For all of us, every hour is grace, every smile a gift.

*Every hour is grace, every smile a gift.*

# NOVEMBER 27

*"The word 'mitzvah' is a commandment to do a good deed.
It's kindling to the soul."*

— Cathie Izen

In the Jewish faith, a *mitzvah* is a good deed. Many Jewish congregations celebrate "Mitvah Day," which is a holiday they have designated to help other people via charitable acts of kindness.

Being kind and helpful is indeed kindling to the soul. Your divine spark is strengthened whenever you love another person and remember that "love" is a verb.

All of us can make mindful mitzvoth (this is the plural of mitzvah) part of our daily routines. After all, when we are helping another person, we are usually actively engaging with them. We are aware of them, and we are alert to their needs and wishes. We are offering ourselves to them in the now.

*I will do good deeds, for they are kindling to my soul.*

# NOVEMBER 28

*"I think 99 times and I find nothing. I stop thinking,*
*swim in silence, and the truth comes to me."*

— Albert Einstein

Focused thought is necessary for certain problem-solving and
detail-oriented tasks. But sometimes focused thought fails us.
No matter how hard we concentrate, we simply can't come up
with the answers we seek. It's a good example of the
limitations of active thought.

You might think that Einstein is advising that exercise can
help us get our thinking unstuck, but no. He couldn't swim!
Here he's talking about metaphorical swimming in silence—
meditation, or non-thought.

When we're stuck on a problem in the now, we can try
meditation or any activity that engages our minds and bodies in
a completely different way. Taking a walk outside, singing along
to a song, chatting with a friend, running errands—anything to
take a break and allow our subconscious to mull over
the problem while we do something else.

In non-thought, the answer often arises as if by magic.

*When I mindfully step outside thought, answers come to me.*

# NOVEMBER 29

*"Creative work is not a selfish act or a bid for attention on the part of the actor. It's a gift to the world and every being in it. Don't cheat us of your contributions."*

— Steven Pressfield

As you grow more acquainted with your divine spark through presence and mindfulness, you will naturally unbury all the creative impulses you've long neglected or denied yourself.

All of us are born with the drive to create. That's why as kids we build sandcastles and forts, make mudpies, and draw drawings. Our culture teaches us that entering adulthood means leaving such childish pursuits behind, so we usually do.

But there are still parts of you that want to bring things into being—and presence and mindfulness require acknowledging and expressing those latent desires. Some of you might want to paint, write, or make pottery. Others of you may have always wanted to learn how to build furniture or bake. Other creative outlets include playing a sport or instrument, learning a foreign language, and decorating a room.

Whatever your creative impulses are, the world needs you to act on them. It doesn't matter how they turn out. It only matters that you be the whole self you came here to be.

*I am creative. The world needs my contributions.*

# NOVEMBER 30

*"Uncertain as I was, I pushed forward. I felt right in my pushing, as if the effort itself meant something."*

— Cheryl Strayed

As you mindfully push forward with your goals, how do you know if you're pushing the right things?

Check in with your intuition. The fear of uncertainty aside, does it feel right? Does it pass the "gut-check" test?

The effort, by the way, does mean something. It's intention in motion. Regardless of whether or not you achieve what you set out to achieve, you're moving in the direction of your passions. This will always take you to the next best place—a new waystation from which you can adjust your plans and if need be, correct or change your course.

We push forward, because the effort itself means something.

*I push forward, because the effort itself means something.*

# DECEMBER 1

*"You do not have to leave the room. Remain standing
at your table and listen.*

*Do not even listen, simply wait. Do not even wait.
Be quite still and solitary.*

*The world will freely offer itself to you to be unmasked.
It has no choice. It will roll in ecstasy at your feet."*

— Franz Kafka

Mindfully, intentionally, regularly practicing stillness
reveals the true world to us.

Falseness falls away. Pretense slinks off. Masks drop.

All we have to do is be quite still and solitary then train our
awareness not on our thoughts but *inside* our thoughts. Life goes
on around us. Our thoughts go on around us. But we remain
still and aware at the center of it all.

From that place of still awareness, we begin to see the eternal.
We begin to connect with the source of all that is and will be.
The universe offers itself to us freely. It has no choice.
It rolls in ecstasy at our feet.

---

*When I am quite still and solitary, the world freely offers itself
to me to be unmasked.*

# DECEMBER 2

*"What day is it?'*

*'It's today,' squeaked Piglet.*

*'My favorite day,' said Pooh."*

— A.A. Milne

The more we are successfully present in our lives, the more
we appreciate that today is always the best day. In fact,
it is only ever the only day.

But is this day really better than, say, a special vacation day?
Or a holiday spent with loved ones?

Or _____?

(Fill in the blank with your favorite way to spend a day.)

Soon we begin to understand that the "better than" question is
the wrong question. The only true question is: When do best
days happen? And the answer is: Today. Always today.

Mindfulness enhances our experience of this day. It opens our
eyes and hearts to all the opportunities for beauty, love, joy,
genuineness, and connection around us. A day filled with these
attributes is surely the best day. Tomorrow will be
another best day too.

*Best days only ever happen today.*

# DECEMBER 3

*"The mind has great influence over the body, and maladies often have their origin there."*

— Jean Baptiste Molière

A recent scientific review of 18 previously published studies has determined that mindfulness can reduce inflammation in the body, which causes or worsens a broad range of illnesses.

The studies looked at people who practice meditation, yoga, breathing exercises, qi gong, and/or tai chi. Researchers found that the mindfulness practitioners had lower levels of inflammatory proteins and fewer other signs of inflammation. Just 15 minutes a day of any mindfulness practice was enough to make a measurable difference.

We're just beginning to truly understand the mind-body connection, but here's some proof that it's more powerful than we often give it credit for. So still yourself and breathe…

*Mindfulness improves my physical health.*

# DECEMBER 4

*"Right in the difficult we must have our joys, our happiness, our
dreams: there against the depth of this background, they stand out;
there for the first time we see how beautiful they are."*

— Rainer Maria Rilke

Like the millions of twinkling stars embroidered on the black
canvas of a cold December night's sky, our joys stand out more
clearly against the backdrop of our sorrows.

Contrast is how we grow to understand many important things.
We may believe a friend is a good friend, for instance, but later,
when we're fortunate to build a relationship with someone whose
daily presence transforms our lives, we understand that the first
friendship was a significant but lesser sort of connection.

Right in the difficult we live our nows. Right in the difficult we
have our joys. We grieve and have gratitude at the same time.

*Right in the difficult I have my joys, my happiness,
and my dreams.*

# DECEMBER 5

*"Mindfulness is the aware, balanced acceptance of the present experience. It isn't more complicated than that. It is opening to or receiving the present moment, pleasant or unpleasant, just as it is, without either clinging to it or rejecting it."*

— Sylvia Boorstein

Sometimes I imagine mindfulness as a sort of mesh screen with really large holes. I hold this screen in front of me, and life passes through it. Random thoughts and feelings flow through. The events of my days flow through.

Significant thoughts, feelings, and events are bigger, so they might get caught in the screen. When this happens, I stop and give them the attention they deserve, eventually freeing them and allowing them, too, to continue on their way.

I don't try to avoid anything that may be coming my direction. Instead, I face everything with a sense of hope, intention, and purpose, head-on, with full awareness, knowing that the screen will help me live each exquisite experience mindfully and genuinely.

With mindfulness, I open to and receive the present moment, just as it is.

*I open to and receive the present moment, just as it is.*

# DECEMBER 6

*"If you were going to die soon and had only one phone call you could make, who would you call and what would you say? And why are you waiting?"*

— Stephen Levine

Tough question.

I'm going to cheat and say I'd send a group text to my family. "I love you more than words can capture," I would type. "You have been my greatest joys. I'm sorry for any times I may have made you feel inadequate or neglected. You are nothing short of miraculous, and if I got lucky enough to do it all over again, I would love you exactly as you are, with full presence, every precious minute I could."

Why am I waiting?

I've gotta go. I have a group text to send. How about you?

*Right this minute, I have a call to make.*

# DECEMBER 7

*"Be happy in the moment. That's enough.*
*Each moment is all we need, not more."*

— Mother Teresa

Here's a great mantra for when you're feeling restless and your
monkey mind keeps spooling out thoughts about what
you lack or what you should be worrying about:

*Everything I need right now is right here.*

You can also reverse it and alternate the two versions:

*Everything I need right here is right now.*

Each moment contains everything sufficient for that moment.
If we are thirsty in the moment, that's OK. It's just a thirsty
moment, and thirsty moments are a normal and natural part of
life. We'll get something to drink in a moment to come.

*This moment is all I need.*

# DECEMBER 8

*"To hurt is as human as to breathe."*

— J.K. Rowling

We hurt whenever something or someone we are attached to is damaged or taken away from us. Since attachment is a natural human tendency, hurt is also a natural human experience.

Being insulted damages our self-esteem. Being ignored damages our hope that we are worthy. Being cheated damages our sense of control and fairness. These (and lots of other principles and beliefs) are all things we're attached to. Hurting them hurts us.

Befriending and embracing our hurt is the most mindful, essential response to it. After all, pain is not bad—it's normal and necessary.

In the now, we can both embrace our pain *and* mindfully call upon our inner knowing that everything is OK. We can grieve and self-soothe. All of this is as human as breathing.

*My hurts are as human as breathing.*

# DECEMBER 9

*"Intuition will tell the thinking mind where to look next."*

— Jonas Salk

Who's in charge—the mind or the soul?

Most of us let our minds run the show. After all, they're the productive, responsible ones. They know what's what. They know what needs doing. They know how to get things done.

Our souls? They're usually wallflowers. They're so quiet we often forget they're there, and they're overly sensitive. Their feelings are hurt too easily.

But when we mindfully quiet the mind and focus more often on inviting the soul to step to the podium, we learn that the soul is the better, truer leader. Where the mind is driven by temporal ego, the soul speaks for the divine, timeless self.

Intuition is the soul's whisper. Listen carefully. Help its voice become louder, and encourage it to train the mind to do its bidding.

*My soul can train my mind to do its bidding.*

# DECEMBER 10

*"Why do they not teach you that time is a finger snap and an eye blink, and that you should not allow a moment to pass you by without taking joyous, ecstatic note of it, not wasting a single moment of its swift, breakneck circuit?"*

— Pat Conroy

Alas, we've wasted a lot of time, you and I. Between us, we've mindlessly blown…what—decades, when you add it all up?

Conroy is right—we're not taught to be mindful. Our culture, educational system, and even some bodies of faith teach us the opposite, in fact. We need to be un-brainwashed.

Our mindlessness ends now. Time passes in a finger snap and an eye blink. We've lost enough already.

From here forward, we commit ourselves to presence. Whenever we catch ourselves living too much in the past or the future, we will return ourselves to the here and now.

*My mindlessness ends now.*

# DECEMBER 11

*"Owning our own story can be hard but not nearly as difficult as spending our lives running from it. ... Only when we are brave enough to explore the darkness will we discover the infinite power of our light."*

— Dr. Brené Brown

In my work as a counselor, I encourage those I am honored to companion to tell me their stories.

Life stories are powerful for many reasons, but one is that the storyteller must, in the telling, find connections that help all the parts and pieces hang together. As they work to tell me their stories, they uncover those key bits of meaning and transition that turn a random sequence of events into a coherent story. Along the way, they grieve and they mourn.

I don't think we can fully inhabit the now until we've fully compiled and owned our own stories. Until then, we're floating, anchorless. We need the tether of reconciliation with our own pasts—no matter how dark or dappled they might be— to not feel the constant pull of the past.

*Only when I am brave enough to explore my darkness will I discover the infinite power of my light.*

# DECEMBER 12

*"Love anything, and your heart will certainly be wrung and possibly broken. If you want to make sure of keeping it intact, you must give your heart to no one, not even to an animal. Wrap it carefully round with hobbies and little luxuries; avoid all entanglements; lock it up safe in the casket or coffin of your selfishness. But in that casket—safe, dark, motionless, airless—it will change. It will not be broken; it will become unbreakable, impenetrable, irredeemable."*

— C.S. Lewis

To protect your heart, love no one. Spend your time and energies on hobbies and little luxuries. In other words, live a shallow life dedicated to things and trivial pursuits. In this mindless and soulless manner, you shall avoid hurt and substantive (i.e., painful) change.

The opposite is what we're working toward, of course. Mindfulness and soulfulness. We are intentionally making ourselves vulnerable. We are giving our hearts to others. We are cutting mindless activities from our lives and replacing them with only mindful endeavors. We seek meaning, connection, and depth, on purpose.

Our hearts will certainly be wrung and possibly broken. We wouldn't have it any other way.

*My heart will be wrung and possibly broken.*
*I will live a meaningful life.*

# DECEMBER 13

*"Instead of cursing the darkness, light a candle."*
— Benjamin Franklin

Here in Colorado, December is dark. When the sun sets at four in the afternoon and doesn't rise again until seven the next morning, it can get a bit depressing. It's easy to fall into despair.

At such times, mindfulness reminds us to light a candle. Whatever brings us joy and fosters hope—those are the things we must intentionally incorporate into our nights of darkness.

Phone calls with faraway friends. Board games. Holding hands with our beloved. Dinners and movies out. Music shows at local venues. Book club. Library events. Adult education classes. Poker night. These and other in-the-now activities are our candles. It's up to us to light them.

*In my darkness, I will light candles.*

# DECEMBER 14

*"My goal is no longer to get more done, but rather to have less to do."*
— Francine Jay

What a good reminder this holiday season. My goal is no longer to get more done, but rather to have less to do.

Overscheduling and overcommitting ourselves is mindless. We can't truly live in the now when we're constantly consulting our to-do lists. We can't appreciate the many wonders of celebrations, friends, and family when we're stressed out and overloaded.

When we simplify, we sometimes have to mourn letting go of old traditions and routines. Yes, it's sad not to bake the traditional family cookies this year. It's a little painful to give up sending holiday cards. But we must remember that it's a trade-off: more living in the now for less "shoulds" and "have tos." More breathing room for fewer trappings.

Better to do a few things mindfully than do a whole lot of things mindlessly.

*With less to do, I can do more things mindfully.*

# DECEMBER 15

*"The person who risks nothing does nothing, has nothing, is nothing, and becomes nothing. He may avoid suffering and sorrow, but he simply cannot learn and feel and change and grow and love and live."*
— Leo Buscaglia

I want to learn and feel and change and grow and love and live. You do too, or you wouldn't be joining me on these pages.

To do so, we've got to regularly take risks. What smallish risks have you taken in the past week? What breathtaking risks have you taken in the past year?

Mindfully build some risk into this day. And the next. And the next. And don't forget to work up to some bigger risks in the coming months. Listen to your intuition, and only take risks that lead in the direction of rewards that are truly meaningful to you.

*I will take risks to learn and feel and change
and grow and love and live.*

# DECEMBER 16

*"Tears are God's gift to us. Our holy water. They heal us as they flow."*
— Rita Schiano

Our bodies produce three kinds of tears.

Basal tears are the natural moisture that bathes our eyes to keep them moist and eliminate bad bacteria. Reflex tears well up when we get something annoying in our eye, like an eyelash or shampoo. And emotional tears rid our bodies of stress chemicals and help us cope with high emotions, sad or happy.

If in the moment we feel like crying, we should trust our bodies and cry. Trying to suppress or deny our tears is not living our present truth. Like all forms of disingenuousness, it's mindless and incongruent.

Tears are God's gift to us. Let them flow.

*When I feel like crying, I will trust my body and I will cry.*

# DECEMBER 17

*"Boredom, anger, sadness, or fear are not 'yours,' not personal.*
*They are conditions of the human mind. They come and go.*
*Nothing that comes and goes is you."*

— Eckhart Tolle

Nothing that comes and goes is you. What falls into that
category? Your looks. Your weight. Your hair (ha-ha). Your job.
Your basic belongings. Your feelings. Your thoughts.
Day-to-day obligations.

What doesn't come and go? Love. Once established, it tends
to stick around, even if the object of that love doesn't. Your
most deeply held values, such as honesty and compassion.
Your personality. The activities and special objects that have the
power to make you gasp with wonder and joy.

The stuff in the first paragraph is temporary. The stuff in the
second paragraph is eternal and thus meaningful. Mindfulness
helps us dedicate more time and awareness each day to the
second paragraph—as well as discern the difference—
so that we don't stress out too much about the first.

*Nothing that comes and goes is me.*

# DECEMBER 18

*"Winter is the time for comfort, for good food and warmth, for the touch of a friendly hand and for a talk beside the fire: it is the time for home."*

— Edith Sitwell

Have you heard of the Danish concept of *hygge*? Pronounced HEW-guh, the term has taken American media by storm lately.

Hygge means, according to the *Oxford Dictionary,* "a quality of coziness and comfortable conviviality that engenders a feeling of contentment or wellbeing."

Curling up on the couch with a blanket, a good book, and a cup of hot tea is hygge. Lighting candles at home and preparing a home-cooked meal with your partner is hygge. Nature is hygge. Natural materials are hygge. Good friends and time spent simply together is hygge.

Hygge is a way of mindfully creating a hospitable ambiance for living in the now. It's fostering presence, pleasure, and affection. What's not to love?

*I will mindfully create a warm, hospitable ambiance for living in the now.*

# DECEMBER 19

*"You have to decide what your highest priorities are and have the courage—pleasantly, smilingly, nonapologetically—to say 'no' to other things. And the way to do that is by having a bigger 'yes' burning inside."*
— Stephen Covey

Learning to say "no" is hard for lots of us. After all, we're working on embracing the now. In the present moment, so many opportunities are available to us. We want to live! We want to help people! We want to engage! We want to say "yes" to all of the possibilities…right?

No, not so much. After all, we can't do everything. There isn't enough time or energy. So we have to use discernment, and we have to mindfully choose.

Every three months I schedule a "Rock Day." I go sit on my favorite rock outside my Center for Loss and ask myself these questions: 1. What am I doing with my time that I no longer enjoy? 2. What am I doing that I really enjoy? 3. What changes do I need to make to my life to ensure I'm spending my time well?

If we mindfully preselect only optional activities that serve our passions and feed our souls, we're on the right track. A gut check serves as a second opinion. Is this something we *want* to do, or is it something we feel we *should* do? Generally, "shoulds" don't belong on our list of highest priorities. Only "yes, I want thats" do.

*I will decide what my highest priorities are and have the courage to say "no" to other things.*

# DECEMBER 20

*"Sometimes you have to let everything go—purge yourself. If you are unhappy with anything—whatever is bringing you down— get rid of it. Because you will find that when you are free, your true creativity, your true self, comes out."*

— Tina Turner

To a large extent, our quest to live in the now is about unencumbering ourselves. Presence requires tuning out the random chatter of our minds and disconnecting ourselves from all the sensory information that isn't essential. It's a process of winnowing and purifying, with the goal of finding meaning and truth.

We purge ourselves in order to find ourselves. As we undertake this housekeeping, we sometimes notice things that make us unhappy. We realize that this person or this activity or this object is not "us" anymore (and maybe never was). Out it goes.

Our newfound clarity frees us. What remains is our true selves.

*I purge myself to find myself.*

# DECEMBER 21

*"The winter solstice has always been special to me as a barren*
*darkness that gives birth to a verdant future beyond imagination,*
*a time of pain and withdrawal that produces something joyfully*
*inconceivable, like a monarch butterfly masterfully extracting itself*
*from the confines of its cocoon, bursting forth into unexpected glory."*

— Gary Zukav

Our darkest times often give birth to our most lush
and transformative growth.

As a grief counselor, I know this, but I also know not to prescribe
it. In the midst of pain, it is not respectful of the pain to talk
about all the good that's going to come out of it. In other words,
living in the now of hurt requires hurting for hurting's sake.

It is necessary to descend before we can transcend.

But when we are ready, and in times of relative calm, it's healthy
to nurture a mindful awareness of the promise of healing and
joy to come. Our pain and withdrawal can indeed produce
something joyfully inconceivable. We gestate in the darkness so
that we can be reborn into the light.

*My darkest times often give birth to my most lush and*
*transformative growth.*

# DECEMBER 22

*"The thing about meditation is: You become more
and more you."*

— David Lynch

Meditation and meditative practices, such as yoga and tai chi,
still the choppy waters of our minds. After all, the waves and
whitecaps are nothing but distractions anyway. They're
show-offs, and like all show-offs, they're falsely self-important.

When the water is perfectly calm, we can see beneath it. What
lies below the water is our souls. *There you are,* we realize.

Meditation makes our true selves visible. Over time, it also
invites our true selves to break through the choppy waters of
our daily lives and lead us in each moment. Turns out our souls
are more powerful than the waves and whitecaps. Through
mindfulness, they breach the waves and sail atop them,
claiming their rightful place as captain of our lives.

*My soul is the captain of my life.*

# DECEMBER 23

*"Unbounded freedom and joy, oneness with the Divine, awakening into
a state of timeless grace—these experiences are more common than
you know, and not far away. There is one further truth, however:
They don't last. Our realizations and awakenings show us the reality
of the world, and they bring transformation, but they pass...
We all know that after the honeymoon comes the marriage.
After the election comes the hard task of governance. In spiritual
life it is the same: After the ecstasy comes the laundry."*

— Jack Kornfield

Especially at first, mindfulness is hard work. No wonder. We
have to completely deprogram and reprogram our minds. But
day by day, we make progress. And one day, we feel ourselves
awakening into a state of timeless grace.

But then something happens, and we lose our balance. We slip
back into mindlessness. We suffer and flail. Or we simply grow
tired of what can seem like the drudgery of living in the now.

When this happens, we can add different kinds of mindfulness
practice to our daily routines. We can also challenge ourselves
in bolder ways. It's a mountain that gets steeper and
steeper as we climb. Onward.

*The ascent to mindfulness gets steeper and steeper as I climb.*

# DECEMBER 24

*"Holiness comes wrapped in the ordinary. There are burning bushes
all around you. Every tree is full of angels. Hidden beauty
is waiting in every crumb."*

— Macrina Wiederkehr

Macrina Wiederkehr is a Benedictine nun and spiritual teacher.
She believes in living in the now with an appreciation for
all the wonders of this world. She also values spending time
in nature. "The book of the earth is as holy as the
book of scripture," she writes.

On this day, let us be on the watch for holiness wrapped in the
ordinary. We can understand holiness as the eternal divine that
inhabits the core of everyone and everything.

As we encounter the holy, let us also stop and express our
wonder and gratitude. What a miracle that we are privileged
to be here to experience all of it.

*I will watch for holiness wrapped in the ordinary.*

# DECEMBER 25

*"Christmas isn't a season. It's a feeling."*

— Edna Ferber

In December, most of us celebrate holidays we find deeply meaningful. The various holidays come to us from different traditions, but they share something essential: a feeling.

Whether we celebrate Christmas, Hanukkah, Kwanzaa, Pancha Ganapati, or any other religious or secular holiday, we feel our holiday in our hearts. We feel love. Hope. Gratitude. Connection with our family and community.

This and all special days, I hope we will be mindful of what we are feeling. Our mindfulness can help us appreciate the profundity of our holidays and also find ways to extend those feelings into regular days.

Through mindfulness, the heightened love, hope, gratitude, and connection we feel now are available to us always.

*Through mindfulness, the heightened love, hope, gratitude, and connection I feel on special days are available to me always.*

# DECEMBER 26

*"Playing is such an important part of our healing process.*
*Our spirit needs to frolic so we can return to innocence."*

— Soo Young Lee

Play is mindfulness's goofy best friend.

It's easy to take mindfulness too seriously. We are present;
we are aware; we are accepting of all that is. We may be at
peace—but are we having any fun?

The remedy for too much Zen-like calm is play. Get silly!
Do something ridiculous!

Play is usually social, involving communion with other people,
and it's often physical, involving our bodies. Living in the now
with others as we move our bodies puts all our wheels
into motion. It's exuberant mindfulness.

Our spirits love to frolic. Let's plan a little frolic into every day.

*Play is exuberant mindfulness. My spirit loves to frolic.*

# DECEMBER 27

*"Energy is the currency of the universe. When you 'pay' attention to something, you buy that experience. … Be selective in your focus because your attention feeds the energy of it and keeps it alive. Not just within you but in the collective consciousness as well."*

— Emily Maroutian

Many of us have been conditioned to value money. We can leverage that conditioning to help us increase our mindfulness.

Thinking of our attention as currency is a quick way to test the true value of an activity. This TV show I'm watching…is it worth the amount of attention I'm paying it? What might I spend this valuable attention on instead?

Our time is an investment. What are we choosing to invest in? Are we mindfully investing in the people and things we care most about? Or are we mindlessly misspending time?

Like a financial investment, what we invest our time in grows, and what we fail to support dwindles.
Mindful investing is wise investing.

*I will invest my time wisely.*

# DECEMBER 28

*"Don't confuse the urgent with the important."*
— Preston Ni

Sometimes in this book we talk about the need to have a sense of urgency. Life is short. That's a reminder that's essential to post somewhere you'll see it often—as in multiple times every day.

But mindful urgency is different than mindless urgency. We run the risk of getting so caught up in the latter that we don't have time for the former.

Email is a good example. It feels urgent, so we try to stay on top of it. But is it important? Ditto social media and the latest popular TV show.

Mindful urgency is about moving ever closer to your important goals and passions, because the clock is ticking. That's the sense of urgency I hope to help you reinforce. The other sense of urgency is nonsense that mindfulness can help us rise above.

*Mindful urgency helps me move ever closer to my important goals and passions.*

# DECEMBER 29

*"We spend most of our lives cutting down our ambitions because the world has told us to think small. Dreams express what your soul is telling you, so as crazy as your dream might seem—even to you— I don't care: You have to let that out."*

— Eleni Gabre-Madhin

Your passions and hopes and dreams express what your soul is telling you.

Your soul doesn't think small. It's here to do great things. It's fear—fostered by social conditioning—that warns you to think small. Ironically, it's your ego that's fearful. Your ego downsizes your hopes and dreams because it doesn't like to take risks, look bad, or feel inadequate.

As crazy as your dreams may seem, they're why you're here. Your soul doesn't think they're crazy, by the way. It's your ego that thinks they're crazy. And your ego is notoriously wrongheaded.

So let your dreams out. All of them. Shepherd them mindfully, and marvel at what unfolds.

*As crazy as they might seem, I will let my dreams out.*

# DECEMBER 30

*"You don't need a new plan for next year. You need a commitment."*
— Seth Godin

After a while, our New Year's resolutions get pretty predictable.
That's because we have the same passions and goals inside us
that we've had for a long time—possibly forever—but
because we haven't pursued them with commitment,
they're still just items on a perennial list.

We probably don't need a new plan. We've already got a plan.
What we need is commitment.

Mindfulness to the rescue!

Mindfulness is like a personal trainer for our souls. It takes our
soul's dreams and goals seriously, and day by day it helps us take
them one step forward. It knows how to work us appropriately
but not too much. It knows how to keep us motivated
and on track. It's got commitment in spades.

*With mindfulness I can commit to my plans.*

# DECEMBER 31

*"Tomorrow is the first blank page of a 365-page book.*
*Write a good one."*

— Brad Paisley

There's something exciting about hanging a new wall calendar.
It's a fresh start. 365 blank squares await our instructions.
It's possibility as far as the eye can see.

With intention, mindfulness, and living in the now, the
coming year can be our best one yet. It's hard to overstate how
dramatically these practices improve our quality of life. Plus,
our improved lives vibrate with such vivacious energy that they
spill over into the lives of those around us, enhancing them too.

Hope is an expectation of a good that is yet to be. I'm hopeful
about the next year. You should be too, because we're
on the same path, and it's a divine one.

Namaste, and Godspeed.

*With intention, mindfulness, and living in the now,*
*the coming year can be my best one yet.*

# A FINAL WORD

Living in the now invites us to surrender to the value of stillness, simplicity, and solitude. Now invites us to seek work-life balance and to trust in the present.

Sadly, these are truths that contemporary culture seems to have forgotten. Societal messages that define "success" often invite us to live completely on the surface.

In contrast, living in the now encourages us to just breathe, to stop engaging in frenetic activity, and to shift our focus to our family, our community, and our God.

Perhaps most importantly, now prepares us to be open to giving and receiving love. Love is the one human experience that invites us to feel beautifully connected to the people around us. Love forces us to acknowledge the magical energy that captures our hearts, nourishes our spirits, and invites us to live in the now.

After you complete a full year with this book, you may want to engage with it again the next year. You will find that as you reread and recommit to the affirmations, they will speak to you in new and different ways. Or if you've found the book helpful during the past 365 days, you may want to pass it along to someone else who is on the path to mindfulness.

My wife, Susan, and I are privileged to be the parents of three young adults, all of whom are now in their twenties. I hope they discover their life callings and muster the courage to pursue them, whatever they are. (Actually, they are well on their way to doing just that). I also hope they relish life's delights, build and nurture loving relationships, and learn to live in the now with both joy and heartbreak.

I hope the same for you. With any luck, we will meet one day, and you can tell me how your mindfulness practice has enhanced your life.

## GRIEF ONE DAY AT A TIME

*365 Meditations to Help You Heal After Loss*

After someone you love dies, each day can be a struggle. But each day, you can also find comfort and understanding in this daily companion. With one brief entry for every day of the calendar year, this little book offers small, one-day-at-a-time doses of guidance and healing. Each entry includes an inspiring or soothing quote followed by a short discussion of the day's theme.

How do you get through the loss of a loved one? One day at a time. This compassionate gem of a book will accompany you.

ISBN 978-1-61722-238-2 • 384 pages
softcover • $14.95

*"Each day I look forward to reading a new page... I can't imagine dealing with my sorrow without [this] book."*

• • • • •

— A reader

ALL DR. WOLFELT'S PUBLICATIONS CAN BE ORDERED BY MAIL FROM:
Companion Press | 3735 Broken Bow Road | Fort Collins, CO 80526
(970) 226-6050 | www.centerforloss.com

# UNDERSTANDING YOUR GRIEF

*Ten Essential Touchstones for Finding Hope and Healing Your Heart*

One of North America's leading grief educators, Dr. Alan Wolfelt has written many books about healing in grief. This book is his most comprehensive, covering the essential lessons that mourners have taught him in his three decades of working with the bereaved.

In compassionate, down-to-earth language, *Understanding Your Grief* describes ten touchstones—or trail markers—that are essential physical, emotional, cognitive, social, and spiritual signs for mourners to look for on their journey through grief.

ISBN 978-1-879651-35-7
176 pages • softcover • $14.95

**The Ten Essential Touchstones:**

Open to the presence of your loss.

Dispel misconceptions about grief.

Embrace the uniqueness of your grief.

Explore your feelings of loss.

Recognize you are not crazy.

Understand the six needs of mourning.

Nurture yourself.

Reach out for help.

Seek reconciliation, not resolution.

Appreciate your transformation.

ALL DR. WOLFELT'S PUBLICATIONS CAN BE ORDERED BY MAIL FROM:
Companion Press | 3735 Broken Bow Road | Fort Collins, CO 80526
(970) 226-6050 | www.centerforloss.com

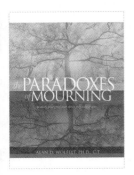

## THE PARADOXES OF MOURNING

*Healing Your Grief with Three Forgotten Truths*

When it comes to healing after the death of someone loved, our culture has it all wrong. We're told to be strong when what we really need is to be vulnerable. We're told to think positive when what we really need is to befriend the pain. And we're told to seek closure when what we really need is to welcome our natural and necessary grief.

The paradoxes of mourning are three Truths that grieving people used to respect but in the last century seem to have forgotten. In fact, our thinking about loss has gotten so mixed up that the Truths can now seem backward, or paradoxical. Yet the paradoxes are indeed true, and only by giving yourself over to their wisdom can you find your way.

*Truth One:* You must say hello before you can say goodbye.

*Truth Two:* You must make friends with the darkness before you can enter the light.

*Truth Three:* You must go backward before you can go forward.

In the tradition of the Four Agreements and the Seven Habits, this compassionate and inspiring guidebook gives you the three keys that unlock the door to hope and healing.

ISBN 978-1-61722-222-1 • 136 pages • hardcover • $15.95

ALL DR. WOLFELT'S PUBLICATIONS CAN BE ORDERED BY MAIL FROM:
Companion Press | 3735 Broken Bow Road | Fort Collins, CO 80526
(970) 226-6050 | www.centerforloss.com